A DALES ODYSSEY

THEN AND NOW

by
HORACE PAWSON
& DENNIS CAIRNS

Aurora Publishing

© Aurora Enterprises Ltd.

Aurora Publishing,
Unit 9C, Bradley Fold Trading Estate,
Radcliffe Moor Road, Bradley Fold,
BOLTON BL2 6RT.
Tel: 0204 370752

ISBN 1 85926 034 9

This edition published 1993

Cover photographs: *(top)* The 'Sturdy Tramps'.
                         (middle) Yockenthwaite, Langstrothdale.
                         (bottom) Horace Pawson, aged 23, from 1913.

Designed, printed and bound by Manchester Free Press,
Longford Trading Estate, Thomas Street,
Stretford, Manchester M32 0JT.

CONTENTS

PREFACE

In July, 1920, less than two years after the First World War had ended, six young men who had experienced the horrors of that conflict decided to spend their one week's annual holiday on foot in the Yorkshire Dales. All were associated with the Wesleyan Methodist Church in Earby, a small town today in Lancashire but then in the West Riding of Yorkshire and most, if not all, were in the church choir. Grassington in Wharfedale was the place chosen at which to begin and end the holiday, this village being no more than twenty miles from Earby. The mode of travel to and from Grassington was by train, something that it is impossible to do today.

Shortly after the six returned from this hike one of their number, Horace Pawson, wrote an account of the holiday which was their first after the war. It went under the rather ponderous title of 'Hill, Dale and Moor; The Adventures of Six Sturdy Tramps'. Certain comments within the account suggest that immediately prior to the war in 1914, a similar holiday had been undertaken. The tale of the 'Sturdy Tramps', as I will often refer to them, is more than a journal simply of where they went or what they did, for it recounts a way of life, customs and habits which have largely disappeared from the Dales. In many instances there is poignancy in the description of scenes and events when the author expresses the joy and thankfulness that they all felt at being able to enjoy simple pleasures which, at one time, they thought they would probably never again experience. There is humour and wit also in some of the anecdotes, whilst certain descriptive points have such a relevance to the life-style and habits of today that one might well ponder on just how far we really have progressed since that time.

Almost three-quarters of a century has now passed since the Sturdy Tramps enjoyed their holiday in the Yorkshire Dales and, in recent years, those who have read Horace Pawson's account of this hike have often asked whether it is possible to follow that same route today. In theory the answer is 'Yes' but perhaps in practice it would not be quite as simple as it was in 1920. A number of rough roads followed by the friends are now metalled highways, albeit not of motorway standard but, nevertheless, used by a considerably greater volume of traffic than was the case over seventy years ago. Certain aspects of public transport which were available to the Sturdy Tramps, most notably some railway services, have long since been withdrawn. On the positive side many of the footpaths and bridleways are much better signed and waymarked than was the case in 1920, whilst the increasing number of visitors to the Dales has ensured that there is available much more overnight accommodation and certainly no shortage of places of refreshment. More than three-quarters of the route traversed by the six friends now lies within the boundary of the Yorkshire Dales National Park and in most of the villages through which their hike took them can be found an information point where one can usually obtain details of local accommodation, some of which invariably changes from one year to the next. This accommodation runs through the whole spectrum from starred A.A. and R.A.C. hotels to bunk barns; from first class self-catering cottages to basic camp sites.

So, during a recent summer, in order to translate theory into practice, my wife and I decided to follow in not too strenuous a fashion, the footsteps of the Sturdy Tramps. At the conclusion of our excursions we were pleasantly surprised to realise just how much of the route still tallied with Horace Pawson's description of seventy odd years ago. Therefore to assist the reader who might wish to do as we did, either as a complete holiday over nine or ten days, or simply to enjoy various stages as individual excursions, complementing Horace's story is an updated commentary on the original route, or alternative paths where necessary, supplemented with information regarding present day rights of way, suggestions for diversions and points of interest to look for and which add a little more colour to one's journey. It is by no means intended to be a detailed and exhaustive description of every footpath, stile, barn and dwelling one might encounter along the way. Plenty of literature on such finer points is already available and a list of some of these publications will be found at the end of this book.

Horace Pawson was born in 1889 and, except for the period during the First World War, lived the whole of his life in Earby or in the neighbouring village of Kelbrook. He left school at the age of twelve and like so many of his contemporaries, his work was that of an operative in one of the local cotton mills. But away from the noise of the looms Horace Pawson enjoyed three main interests, all of which are embodied in the story; his fondness for music, his devotion to the Methodist Church and, above all, that of the amateur naturalist. In pursuit of this hobby he walked thousands of miles and conveyed his love of the countryside to many people through his extensive knowledge of the wildlife he observed and studied on his numerous hikes. He died in 1956 and the account which follows, written originally in four exercise books, is being published without any alterations except for the title and with the full co-operation of his surviving son, Bernard Pawson, to whom I am indebted for his help.

As one who has enjoyed a long acquaintanceship with many of the Yorkshire Dales, the impact of 'The Adventures of Six Sturdy Tramps' through the descriptive writing of its author has opened my eyes and indeed all my senses to much that previously I had given little thought or simply allowed to pass un-noticed. I hope that it will do the same for you.

Dennis Cairns, 1993.

ACKNOWLEDGEMENTS

In preparing this volume I spoke to various people, names unknown, in the Dales villages who gave me an insight into life as it was and as it is today. To these folks I express my thanks, as I do to the curator of the Reeth Folk Museum for clarifying the mystery regarding Horace Pawson's 'Blue Bell' Inn. The exercise books in which the original account was written contain numerous picture postcards of early 20th Century vintage as well as a few original photographs, some of which are repro-duced here. I am grateful to Mr. D. Swires of Summerbridge for allowing me to include the two photos relating to Scar Village and Lofthouse station in Nidderdale. Other photographs and maps are my own contribution. Finally, I must admit to a strong family connection in producing this book, since Horace Pawson was uncle to my wife Grace, who supported me in all weathers on my various excursions, whilst my younger son Peter, contributed the sketches. To both go my most sincere thanks

D.C.

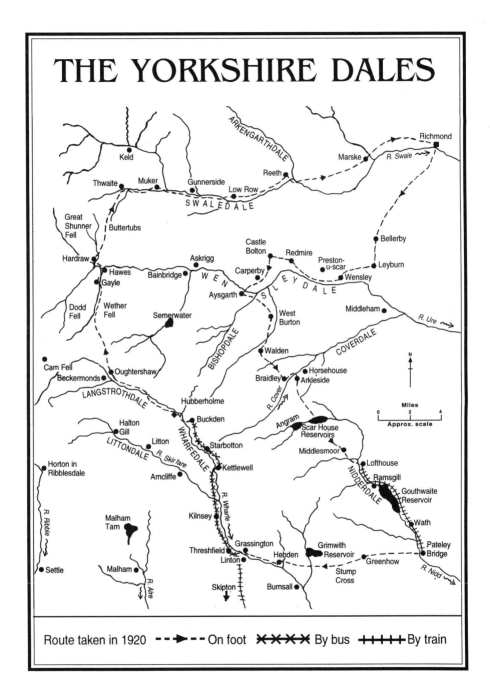

THE YORKSHIRE DALES

Route taken in 1920 --►--- On foot ✕✕✕✕ By bus ┼┼┼┼ By train

The Sturdy Tramps......
Who Were They?

From left to right: Harry Bailey (Sergeant-Major), Wellbury Holgate (Private/Lance-corporal), Alec Eastwood (Junior Major), Alfred Astin (Corporal), Rennie Pawson (Colonel), Horace Pawson (Adjutant Major).

PART ONE

THE ODYSSEY — AS IT WAS

1920

INTRODUCTION

At the outset let me state that I give the following simply as a record of our experiences during an ideal holiday and not in any sense as a feat of pedestrianism, for one hundred miles in eight days would rank insignificant as a record breaking attempt. I hope that that which I now write will, in after years, afford me and others much pleasure in perusal.

It was finally settled that we should go on a walking tour for our holidays, six of us all told. We all assumed military titles such as colonel, major (adjutant), major (junior), sergeant-major, corporal and private. Irrespective of rank, each carried his belongings in a bulging ruck-sack and it was obvious from the start that everyone had got the "hump".

For the benefit of those persons who wonder what we carry in these bags of mystery, I will briefly give a short list describing the average contents. Most important of all, a change of clothing will be most appreciated after a hot walk; flannel trousers, shirt, singlet, slippers, two or three pairs of socks, collars and tie. Next, shaving tackle, towel, soap, handkerchiefs, brush and comb, drinking cup, cycle cape or army mac. I should say that the foregoing are necessaries and if comfort is to be considered at all they could hardly be dispensed with. We also carried other impedimenta such as songs and song books, camera and army dixie, but as this latter was used only once it will not be included on our next trip. Thus our packs varied in weight from eight to thirteen pounds which is easily carried in a ruck-sack without undue exertion.

H. Pawson.

*Top: Horace Pawson,
aged 23, 1913.
Right; Horace c.1955.*

DAY ONE . . . SATURDAY

GRASSINGTON HAWES

In military parlance we had fixed Grassington Station as our 'jumping-off point', but as the weather turned out very vile we decided to make Buckden our point of vantage, the intervening ten miles we did by charabanc. On alighting from the vehicle we donned our capes and proceeded along the Hawes road to the little hamlet of Hubberholme where we found food and shelter at the hostel called the George Inn.

Here we were joined by a Wesleyan Choir party who came from Thornton near Bradford. We had already become acquainted with several members of this same party at Skipton Station. Our host of the inn, a typical 'Boniface', chock full of wit and racy anecdotes of the Dales and of which he has the gift of narration. Afterwards, we found that he dearly loved a song and on one occasion tears were observed in his eyes. He is an elderly man. In stature about five feet six inches, rather round faced and of swarthy countenance; his eyebrows are dark and bushy and his brown eyes have in them a mischievous twinkle. On his head is a close-fitting cap, rather awry; he is in his shirt sleeves and without collar; he is dressed in knee-breeches and his ample calves are covered with coarse woollen stockings. His feet are encased in enormous clogs.

Attentive to the wishes of several thirsty individuals who quaff strange liquors, his ironshod feet are continually clattering over the stone-flagged floor. In one corner sits an old farmer evidently deep in his cups, occasionally sipping with a philosophical air of contentment. A young red-faced coach driver enters and a drink is ordered. This he swallows at a gulp, never even smacking his lips at the operation. Surely he cannot have tasted it! Yet he is apparently satisfied and he takes his departure. Another ruddy-featured man performs the vanishing trick with drink after drink and he is getting rather merry. In an adjoining room is heard the strains of an Irish jig; also girlish laughter with the remark, "I allus liked wimmin better nor men!" The old farmer rises from his corner, a tall figure, six feet four

4

The landlord of the 'George Inn'.

inches. He walks with bent head and enters the little parlour and there we see him capering to and fro jigging to the time of the music, much to the amusement of the ladies.

Amongst such scenes as these we do full justice to the homely fare set before us; new homemade bread, cheese and new laid eggs. Though our host is a dispenser of 'throat gargles', be it noted that he is a man with business instincts and never drinks in his own house. Besides being farmer and inn-keeper, he is sexton of the little church across the way, of which he is justly proud and from him we obtain the keys of this quaint structure. In a high-pitched voice he tells us how he once had to refuse these same keys to a traveller who wanted to sleep the night in the church. "No!" he informed him, "we doan't let onyb'dy sleep i' t' church, we nobbut let 'em sleep i' t' churchyard!"

He also informs us that "up t' Dale, fooak sometimes forget day o' t' week and when this 'appens t' Buckden bobby goes up ter tell 'em when it's Sunday, sooas they'll knooa when ter corm ter t' church!"

Leaving his genial company for a few minutes, we visit the church

5

across the lane. At this juncture we think that we could not do better than quote Waddington's description of the place.

"The church still retains its ancient rood-loft, dated 1558, the work of a carpenter named William Jake. A plain cross, erected about fifty years ago, has taken the position of the rood or image of Christ. The great deluge of 1696 flooded the church and left fish from the Wharfe inside on the waters receding. To keep out floods, the Normans had added a substantial porch. The bell (1603) has Queen Elizabeth's monogram and the motto, 'Jesu be our speed'. She died on the 24th March in that year and it is quite possible that this is a memorial bell. Over the principal porch is the motto, 'A Sunday well spent brings a week of content', and on one of the walls, 'Be the day short or be the day long, at last cometh the evensong'. St. Michael's Church possesses only one ancient brass. It belongs to the Tennants, is dated 1775 and commemorates a mother's lament over her fourteen year old son:

When full of years and bending to the tomb,
His earthy race well run,
Man meets his doom: wailing at first his loss
At length we find some solace in the fame he leaves behind.
But when a youth of goodliest hopes appears,
His virtues growing with his growing years,
Who, in his dawn, each fluttering sign puts forth
Each fairest promise of a day of worth.
When such appears and perishes so soon,
Birth of a morning — brushed away at noon,
Who would not grieve from so severe a blow?
Judge then, a mother's unutterable woe. . ."

Hubberholme is supposed to be derived from 'Hubba' who was a Danish commander at the time the Danes held the City of York, and 'holme' means meadowland or pasture by a river. In visiting these old sanctuaries, one is always impressed by the solemnity and sacredness of the surroundings. Reverently we walk the aisles and converse in subdued tones.

Here, within these grey walls where generations of worshippers have assembled, it seems the very air has become pregnant with worship and it makes one wonder if the spirits of the departed still pervade the holy place.

Hubberholme Church, Rood Screen.

Standing in the choir we sing several hymns of evensong, 'Abide with me', 'Lead kindly light' and others.

Outside, our friend the innkeeper is yarning to an amused audience: "There's chapel ower Hebden Brigg way, where ye hev ter goa up steps ta get inta t'bottom and down steps to get inta t'gallery. I dare say I've bin theer hundreds o'times misel. One chap thowt he'd like to be a local prearcher, so they let 'im try. He oppened t'service and read a lot out o' t'Bible, then after a bit he gev out 'is text, 'I am the Good Shepherd', but he couldn't goa ony further. Then he gev out another hymn and began agean, 'I am the Good Shepherd'. Agean 'is tongue stuck and one of 'is mates fra t'congregation shouts out, "I say Bill, coom daan here, tha'll mak a better sheep nor a shepherd!"

Our choir from Thronton now sang the hymn 'Praise ye the Lord' to the tune 'Rimington'. Our listeners included the landlady, neatly dressed in manner ladylike with a speech not of these parts. By her side is her maid, a typical Dales lassie from Hawes, fresh and fair to look upon and true to type. We shall see a likeness in every Dales maid we meet, for her environment has left its impression. She savours of the churn and the cheese-press and household duties are a second nature to her. Like sailors, these dales-people have in their eyes that faraway expression that comes of looking upon distant objects. Here we have the sinuous mountain track fading away into the distance, the river, distant contours of mountain and rugged fell and miles and miles of billowy heathland devoid of habitation. Among such surroundings it is, therefore, not surprising that we get a 'type' or a change in physiognomy.

Again the old farmer has forsaken his glass for another glance at the 'wimmen'. Perhaps he too finds something attractive in another type of female beauty from the towns. Who knows? Meanwhile, sexton-farmer-innkeeper's dog has been pawing our waistcoats with his dirty paws, but he comes to heel at his master's, "Come ahint, Jack, ye red heead!" We now make our adieus and our host says, "If ye see owt o' some cows a piece on t'way, ye might just turn ther heeds this way." We promise!

Following the course of the Wharfe upstream above Buckden, it takes a sudden turn westwards, whence it flows from a beautiful valley called Langstrothdale. We follow the road on its left bank until we come to Yockenthwaite where a bridge spans the foaming torrent. Today the current is very swift and the nut-brown waters tumble grandly over rocky ledges into deep pools of inky blackness. Opposite to where a number of ducks are gathered by the water, a farm lad comes through a gateway when the following dialogue ensues.

"Now, my lad, how much do you want for one of your ducks?"

"Them ducks isn't mine," he answered.

"Whose ducks are they?" we ask.

"They belong to Kit Hayes at t'Hillside Farm," he said.

"Well you might sell us one," we persisted. "We'll give you four bob for one."

"I tell yer, they're not mine, but if yer want one yer can take one!"

Here the corporal produced an official looking notebook and asked the lad his name as a guarantee. But the little fellow was unimpressed by this show of bluff. He stood before us, a sturdy figure with legs wide apart, both hands deep in top trousers pockets, cap jauntily set on one side of his head, shirt loose at the neck.

"My name's James Sellers. Gi' me t' four bob and ye can take what ye like!" he stoutly asserted.

On our approach, Farmer Hayes' ducks again breasted the buff coloured water of the swollen river and quacked defiantly.

The valley now becomes deeper and more narrow and the fells rise steeply on each side, surface broken with ridge and hollow. Scattered about are the black-faced fell sheep quietly browsing on the somewhat scanty herbage through which the grey limestone peeps in places. We pass an isolated farmhouse and a shepherd's dog barks at us across the stream. Where a letter-box is built into the wall we pass through a gate and observe a few scattered houses and farm buildings which denote the world's-end hamlet called Beckermonds.

Our road now diverges to the right up a rather stiff hill and, as rain is beginning to fall, we don our capes and walk rather quickly for the next half-mile. On our left, snugly situated in the valley below, is Oughtershaw Hall. Today it has rather a forbidding appearance in its setting of dark pine trees. The rain is now coming down in earnest and we take shelter under a mountain ash whose spreading branches overhang a little limestone cliff by the roadside. Here also is a well of nice fresh water and a stone seat and for the meantime we are fairly sheltered from the rain. Above the well is a bronze tablet let into the rock which is inscribed with the following:

"In remembrance of their mother's first visit to Oughtershaw, 12th August, 1853. This well was placed by her son, Charles H. L. Woodd and Lydia, his wife. 'Whosoever drinketh of this water shall thirst again.' — John, ch.4, v.13. 'If any man thirst let him come unto me and drink.' — John, ch.7, v.37."

Whilst we are resting and as we shall shortly be leaving Wharfedale, a few words about that river would not come amiss. Just below Beckermonds two streams come into confluence; these bring down the headwaters from Cam Fell, 1,800 feet, where both originate, very few yards intervening between their sources and the springs of the Ribble. These streams are known as the Green Field Beck and Oughtershaw Beck. Throughout its length of sixty miles, until it reaches the Ouse at Cawood, the Wharfe has rather a rapid flow and it is turbulent at flood times. When in flood, places like Linton Falls and the Strid at Bolton Woods are well worthy of a visit. Truly, it is a river of moods; one day it glides serenely along, a crystal stream, wherein the brown trout leap and the minnows play hide and seek in the shallows. The next day it is full to overflowing and the amber coloured-flood rushes along with fleecy-white foam caps riding its troubled surface. The river rises suddenly for its drainage area is enormous. From the fells of Barden and Buckden and a great stretch of country from Coverhead to Pen-y-Ghent come the tributaries, for here rises the Skirfare

Hawes, Mill Stream, 1920.

which drains Littondale and joins forces with the Wharfe below Kettlewell. Reared amongst the mighty fells 'tis no weakling that sets out seaward, and the scenery along its banks is splendid.

We sit watching the rain sweeping across the valley but now our rowan, above, has commenced to drop aqueous streamlets down our necks. Presently there is an abatement and the shower has nearly passed. We now make our way past little Oughtershaw, a lonely outpost of civilisation, and face a mountainous rampart of fells. Here we begin to climb. The road or pass leads between Dodd Fell, 2189 feet and Wether Fell, 2,015 feet, at one place the actual road reaching 1,850 feet. On our right we catch a glimpse of two rather pretty cascades falling in a grandeur of foam and spray. A strong light seems to penetrate the clouds, striking the valley we are leaving. We look and see the Oughtershaw Beck in its meanderings down the vale from its cradle on Cam Fell. Now, we are in a bank of clouds drifting across our path. Through this filmy curtain, black peat stacks stand out like lonely sentinels on the moor and the road ahead fades into nothingness. We top the summit at last and enter Wensleydale. The descent is begun, the clouds lift, patches of blue appear and the sun is on us once more. We hail the coming of 'Sol' with a cheer. All are right glad of the chocolate ration which the private now issues. Commissioned and non-commissioned officers are loud in his praises and promotion never looked nearer than at this moment when the colonel beamed upon him. To good old marching tunes we tramp down the road into the land of cheeses and waterfalls:

'Tis the open road for me,
Where I wander fancy free.
Away to the purple hills,
Or down to the dancing sea
Far over the moor it bends,
Down the smiling vale descends,
And all whom I pass, I greet,
For every face is a friend's.

The gossips of Gayle watch us pass through their quiet old village which is the very antithesis of its name. Here the limestone strata is seen in horizontal beds and the step-like appearance of the river bed is most remarkable. All around us are great hills with crests of limestone scars,

Hawes, The Crown Hotel, 1920.

meadows and pasture land, river and copse. On turning a corner we sight Hawes, our destination for the day. Walking up the spacious main road, we come to the Crown Hotel where, fortunately, we obtain lodgings for the night. Here, according to the old farmer at Hubberholme, we should have "good beds and plenty of grub and tiger!"

We were much puzzled to know what he meant by 'tiger' but afterwards we discovered he meant pig and a fine flavoured meat we found it. We sampled it at breakfast next morning. The evening we spend in sauntering about the little town. Resting on a seat, we watch the simple amusements of the young people playing together in real, old, country fashion. Then after business hours, we adjourned to the comfortable private drawing room at the 'Crown', where we had a sing-song and our colonel tickled the ivories in fine style. It was here where we obtained our catch phrase for the week. A young man entered the room who evidently had imbibed too deeply during the evening and even yet his thirst was not quenched. In thick, beery tones he says, "Now then, wodjer-going'-to-have?" He seems strangely nonplussed when we do not respond to his request, for a refusal is, to him, a novel experience. "Nay, d. . . it all, we can't go on like this!" he ejaculates. "Wodjer-goin'-to-have? Wodz yours?" In the morning he had a thick head but said he would be all right in two or three days!

DAY TWO . . . SUNDAY

HAWES TO MUKER

In the visitors" book we left our illustrious names with the following verse, one composed for the occasion by the junior major:

'Over the hill from Hubberholme
We wended our weary way,
But rest we found as the sun went down
In the "Crown" at the end of the day.
We are the boys of Earby Town,
Who hold serenade when the lights go down.
Some of us are ginger and some of us brown,
But we're all very spruce in the morning.'

'Healthy Hawes' as it is called is situated 800 feet above sea level and is the second highest market town in England. It has a population of about 1,600. The air is fresh and invigorating whilst the scenery is delightful. In the vicinity there are numerous cascades and waterfalls of extraordinary beauty and shortly we shall visit one of them. Sunday morning turned out very cloudy but after a while the clouds scattered and there were prospects of a fine day. There was blue sky visible; the sun shone warmly. Presently, after a few verses of "Rimington", we shouldered our bags and made for open country, just when other people were making for church. We cross the Ure near the cricket field and proceed through the fields to Hardraw. Be it here noted that Wensleydale takes its name from the picturesque village of Wensley and not from the river as in most other dales. Arriving at Hardraw we obtain permission to visit the famous Scaur Fall. For this privilege we pay fourpence each and obtain the key from an inn, "The Green Dragon". Entering the gorge we leave the key in the lock as we shall return this way. A stony path leads up to and behind the fall. Today there is a huge volume of water which plunges over the edge of rock 100 feet above. Striking the pool below with a deafening roar, it becomes a seething mass of foam and the air is filled with spray. Beyond description, there is a subtle grandeur about a waterfall and we watch with a strange fascination the falling water. Time and again our eyes turned from the edge of the precipice to the cauldron below, vainly trying to follow some imaginary piece of water in its downward journey. Here is power, unceasing energy, a mighty titanic hammer ever at work. We are impressed by its strength and are reminded of the words 'Men may come and men may go, but I go on for ever'. For countless ages this relentless force has been at work, ever eating the softer strata below the harder rock and for unnumbered years to come this process of disintegration will continue. In aeons, dim and distant, when we are reincarnated, it will be interesting to visit this place and see how denudation has progressed! We reach the top of the cliff by a series of steps, we cross the stream by a footbridge and regain the Buttertubs road immediately. For the first two miles it is rather a stiff climb; with our ruck-sacks and other impedimenta it is warm work in the heat of the blazing sun and we perspire freely. At little rills, drinking cups are in evidence and the sergeant-major leers and asks, "Now, wodjer-goin'-to-have? Wodz yours?"

Near the summit of the pass on the high side of the road, tall posts are placed at intervals. These are intended to guide the unlucky travellers who, perchance, traverse this bleak region when snow has obliterated all vestiges of a road. We call a halt where a little stream issues from a rocky hollow on the hillside. Several rabbits scurry away on our approach and whilst the others sit down, the junior major and the private make gallant but futile attempts to unearth the animals by removing rocks. Had they not been so absorbed in their labours, they might have heard the chuckles of one bunny who had come out to view operations from the rear. She was very much amused to see their attempts to move mountains and it was only when the private disappeared head first down a hole that she really became alarmed about the safety of her young, and vanished.

It was a day of clear views. Looking back, we observed flat-topped Ingleborough and the rounded mass of Whernside in the distance; to our left we see Dodd Fell and Wether Fell with the road we traversed yesterday winding like a white ribbon up the hill. Then a vision of Upper Wensleydale in the foreground. The great fell slopes form a huge gully and beyond is Great Shunner Fell, 2,340 feet, with cloud shadows creeping up its rugged green flanks. Behind us, Lovely Seat, 2,215 feet, and rocky limestone scars. Up packs and we're on the road again. The newly clipped mountain sheep stare inquisitively at us as we enter their domain. A long undulating track is this fell road amid the desolate bogland. We are now descending; the road is built on the steep side of a rock-strewn valley. There are precipitous, jagged fissures in the limestone, varying from forty feet to sixty feet in depth, formed, like the potholes of Ingleborough, by the percolating action of water charged with carbonic acid which acts as a solvent on the limestone, each drop carrying off a particle of carbonate of lime in solution. Cautiously, we walk round the edges of the chasms and peer into their gloomy depths. In places, the rocky aspect has been softened by the plants, ferns and shrubs which have found a habitat and flourish in the most inaccessible places. From below comes the rather musical tinkle of water dripping into a hidden pool. After our camera friend has risked the exposure of a plate, we move down the winding road into Swaledale. Again, the view is magnificent, everywhere great hills rear their rocky crests. On the lower slopes, rough stone walls mark the division of the fields and we are struck by the number of little out-houses that are dotted about on the hillsides, reminding us very much of block-houses. We speculate on the reason for having these small barns and presume it is to save the farmer the trouble of taking hay a long distance. Transport on these steep fell sides is not easy matter and the horse-drawn sledge is in common use.

Upper Swaledale is not as well wooded as Upper Wensleydale, but its scenery is of a more rugged type and possesses characteristics of its own. But further downstream the two dales are very similar in appearance.

The day is very hot and we are hungry, dinnertime having gone by an hour. We meet a youth perspiringly pushing a bicycle up the roughest part of the road. We give him encouragement in his labours and, later, see him a silhouetted figure on the skyline. Bravo! Excelsior! Further along, a pedlar and his wife are busy peeling potatoes for dinner in true Bohemian fashion by the roadside. We reach a little place called Thwaite and obtain dinner at the Temperance Hotel there, a place we can recommend for good, wholesome food. Thwaite, like some of its neighbours, has seen more prosperous times, when lead mining was the occupation of its inhabitants. Then, the value of that mineral depreciated and the mines were closed in consequence. The miners were obliged to leave and cottages have long been unoccupied and now fallen into ruin. But now that lead has risen in

"— a pedlar and his wife are busy peeling potatoes —"

price, there is again talk of reopening the mines. We should be pleased to see this place restored to its former beauty. May the time not be far distant when trim gardens replace a wilderness of weeds and homely cottages rise from the ruins of the old. A peaceful, old-time village, this Thwaite among the giant hills slumbering in solitude with a singing brook that croons its song of lullaby the whole day through. Restfulness permeates the very atmosphere and we are influenced by the feeling. Three of the company are spread full length on a fine, home-made hearthrug, while another disports himself in an ungainly attitude on a wooden bench by the door. After we have disposed of the victuals, we sing several well-known hymns. It is here that we find the tune 'Beautiful Zion' which was new to us but which a Pateley Bridge gentleman said his mother used to sing him to sleep, to the words 'Rock-a-bye baby on a tree top'. We are loth to leave but soon wend our way down a pleasant lane tinged with the bright blue of the meadow geranium and the varied tints of the wild rose.

On arriving in Muker, and because they had the cleanest faces, the adjutant and the sergeant-major were detailed off to get lodgings and they successfully induced Mrs. H. to accept us as guests for the night. The adjutant and the private stayed at Mrs. H.'s and the other officers with the corporal adjourned to a nice little cottage across the way. Later, we will

Muker from the south.

view the interior. We wash, shave, and anoint our hair with sweet smelling oils, and soon we are enjoying a refreshing cup of tea in the cool parlour. A few minutes' walk up the road is the little Methodist chapel. Thither we make our way to the service which should commence at seven o'clock. We are there fifteen minutes before the time but the doors are closed. At five minutes to seven a white-bearded old gentleman, soberly dressed in black, comes towards us. He greet us, 'Good evening'; we return his salutation and make various remarks about the weather. At two minutes before seven a body of people approach from the direction of the village. These, with the exception of a few stragglers, compose the whole congregation and the service commences five minutes late. Never have we seen an audience assemble so quickly. The choir is composed of three young ladies, two little girls and a solitary bass! Needless to say, there was no anthem. We had an able discourse from a young man who had come seven miles to fulfil his appointment! The singing is good and we enjoy the service immensely. The sun is sinking behind a high hill and the shadows are creeping across the valley as we saunter down the lane and through the little village. It is a beautiful evening, cool and calm, and the air is perfumed with the scent of wayside flowers. In the snug little cottage we exercise our vocal organs in song. We have an audience of old and young.

A little girl with a delightfully sweet voice signs the last verse of 'Abide With Me' as a solo. It was divine.

Mrs. H. has a young lady visitor whom the junior major has gallantly escorted to the cottage. They now enter and the young lady sits by the side of the sergeant-major in the cosy three-seat inglenook, the junior major following with the intention of occupying the vacant seat. But he is forestalled by the private who dashes in and secures the coveted seat by the lady. A scene is avoided, but a steely glint comes into the eyes of the junior major that bodes ill for the private. Had that individual not been so engrossed in his attentions to his fair partner, he would have felt more uncomfortable under the junior major's prolonged and bitter gaze. Later the private gave us a further sample of his audacity when we walked to Mrs. H.'s for supper, his left arm intertwined with that of the young lady of the inglenook. Can we wonder at the junior major's wrathful countenance? There is no need to enlarge on the fact that we had a good supper, or that we slept well. Neither will we dwell on the fact that it was the private who, in the morning, entered the officers' quarters by the bedroom window and aroused those gentlemen from sleep. But the court martial we must not omit to mention, else our record of this holiday would not be complete.

DAY THREE . . . MONDAY

MUKER TO REETH

The court martial occurred immediately after we had settled our bill. At the head of the long mahogany table sat the colonel of austere expression, drumming the table with his slender fingers. The junior major sat with his back to the piano, a complacent smile overspreading his face. In the corner is the adjutant, smoking a cigarette. At the colonel's command. "Bring in the prisoner!" a crunch of hob-nailed boots is heard on the cobbles outside and strident tones of "Left, righ'!" are heard. The prisoner enters with full kit, in charge of the sergeant-major and the corporal. "Halt! Righ' turn!" He turns smartly and faces the colonel.

Colonel: "What is this man charged with?"

Sergeant-major: "He is charged with conduct prejudicial to the good discipline of the troops." And to the private, "Stop your laughing!"

Colonel: "Give me the outstanding facts of the case."

Between them, the sergeant-major and the junior major give a graphic account of the happenings of the previous evening concerning the girl of the inglenook, enlarging if anything on the actual affair. The colonel is looking very stern. "Have you anything to say why this charge should not be brought against you" he asks. The private opens his mouth to speak when the colonel points his finger at him, "Shut up, man! No insolence, mind you."

He then turns to the junior major. "Who is this female referred to, junior major?"

"Sir, she is a darling. . ."

Here the colonel almost explodes with wrath. "Sir, I really must ask you to be more careful in the choice of language!"

"I'm sorry," replies the junior major. "What I was going to say, sir, is that she is from Darlington, a Darlington girl."

The colonel now looks through the private. "Private W., you have been charged and found guilty of a most despicable offence. You have flouted your superior officers and caused discord in the ranks. It is my intention to deal with this and, indeed, all similar cases with the greatest severity. In passing through towns and villages I must ask all officers and N.C.O.'s to exercise the utmost vigilance and caution, and report direct to me any cases of laxity of conduct or discipline amongst the troops. It is my determination to eradicate all vestiges of insubordination among the rank and file. I am determined to keep unsullied the fair name of this portion of the British Army under my command. Ahem! Therefore, I warn you private, er. . .Private W. that your sentence will not be light. I award you forty-eight days F.P.No.1 and to carry my pack for the rest of this day. Sergeant-major, your escorts; away with the prisoner!"

Sergeant-major: "Prisoner, 'shun! Righ' turn, by the left, quick march march!"

In passing, we are glad to report that by attention to duty, the private earned a remission of practically the whole of his sentence, and further, before our march ended he had earned his first stripe.

Outside, the morning air is fresh and sweet and a faint aromatic scent of burning peat hangs in the atmosphere. We stand chatting with Mr. H. who is just going to feed his poultry. Nearby is the little village institute, built about sixty years ago. He takes us into the upper room where hundreds of leather-bound books are ranged along dust-covered shelves. He observes us admiring the binding of a heavy tome and assures us that we couldn't get a book 'bun' like that nowadays. Indicating a three-quarter size billiard table, he says, "This is what pays now. We get this place full nearly every night. We again look round at the rows of books which, by appearances, are seldom if ever disturbed, and cannot but lament if the youth of Muker have foresaken books for billiards, always remembering that a craze for anything is to be deplored, even for reading. We cannot help but think that the books would be read more if they were 're-bun' in a more attractive case. There are some good volumes amongst them but in their present drab coverings we would, somehow, not be tempted to read them. We could say more about the cheerful binding of books, but we now go outside again. From a farmhouse up the road comes the rattle of milk-cans which are being placed outside to sweeten, and their burnished sides shimmer in the sunlight. Down the hillside, opposite, comes a little pony ridden by a girl and led by another. Both wear white sun-bonnets and look very picturesque. Presently, they pass us and smile at us familiarly. The pony also carries two small milk-kits strapped on a wooden pannier. The schoolmistress now arrives on her bicycle and children pass us on their way to school. The village post office does a roaring trade in stamps and postcards. One of the party went in when the post—mistress was speaking through the telephone, which was fixed out of sight. "Hullo!" someone shouted when he entered. "Hullo!" he responded.

"Do you want local?" the voice continued.

"Yes, views of Muker, please," he answered unconcernedly.

"Hullo! Yes, two and four a pound. Right! Will see you tomorrow," went on the voice. Then the lady emerged from behind the partition and he found out his mistake! Before we depart, we have the usual sing and then bid goodbye to the kindly Mr. and Mrs. H. and their charming visitor. Here the junior major has more inspiration:

'With the morning light we are merry and bright,
And high our glasses we raise.
With a hale goodwill, we drink our fill,
Our kindly hostess praise.'

In spite of what the colonel had said about the private having to carry his pack, he absentmindedly carries it himself, much to the relief of the private. Down the road we discover that we have forgotten the camera and the songbook. The junior major and the private volunteer to return for the same! Just below Muker, a deep valley indicates the passage of the Swale flowing from pretty Keld, a sequestered hamlet at the head of the dale. We are sorry to miss this rare beauty spot with its fine cataracts and its rural pleasantness. Down the vale we follow the charming country lane, up hill and down, with a fresh view at every turn of the road. From among the grasses on the steep meadow sides, the giant scabious rears his purple head. By the wayside are beds of snowy bedstraw and the musk smelling crosswort. Occasionally are seen the pale blue spikes of the spotted orchid and the yellow flowers of St. John's Wort. The stately blue campanula has commenced to open its bell-like blossoms and offers open invitation to nectar-loving insects. Rose bushes are a dream of beauty with gorgeous sprays of red, white and pink. The sun's rays are beating down on us and a swarm of flies persistently follows our perspiring heads. Again and again, we flick them off, for their presence irritates us. Instead of attacking them, we adopt defensive measures and cover our heads with handkerchiefs, a method which proves successful. They can now indulge in free rides if they so wish. Speaking about flies, there is one particular species which seems very fond of Swaledale. In the hot summer of 1914, we met him in large numbers here. We remember how a flat rock by the roadside (nearly a yard square), was literally one moving mass of buzzing flies. Not caring to investigate too closely their attraction for the stone, we had the joy of putting many of the swarm hors-de-combat by throwing stones at them. He is a vicious looking creature with a long, grey body varying in length from half an inch to one inch. His wings are mottled grey. He is armed with a long, sharp, corkscrew lancet with which he easily pierces one"s skin. This weapon must be long in comparison to his body, for we have seen him make a horse kick with the pain of the bite. But the 'corkscrew' is his down fall when dealing with human beings, for once let him commence operations it is safe to predict his death if our smite is sure. Then we have the satisfaction of gloating over his ugly carcass! We do not know his proper name, but he is known to us as the 'Clegg' or horse-fly. Wherever flies go in wintertime, we would consign this brute to regions far hotter than any on earth, if we had our way.

At a well of cold, fresh water, we wash our hands and wrists. The appearance of a drinking cup brings forth the remark, "Now, colonel, wodz yours? Wodjergointohave?" The sight of two of the party 'taking the waters' is too funny to be missed and a charming photograph is obtained, although we do not expect it will be hung in the Royal Academy. On our left, nestling at the foot of a great hill, is the village of Gunnerside. Instead of following the road to this place, we continue along a sequestered grass-grown lane by the right bank of the river. A perfume of aniseed is borne to us on the breeze and presently we discover the origin of the scent to be a large bed of sweet cicely which someone has cut to the ground. We greatly appreciate its fragrance. We love these dustless old lanes with hedgerows green as Nature intended. We believe their freshness and quietude is good for the soul, a perfect Paradise in comparison to the modern highway with its stream of flying vehicles, the stench of burnt gases from exhaust valves and the nerve-wracking sound of warning hooters. In a shallow reach of the river, we wade; the water is very cold but refreshing. Here, several horse-flies come after our blood but they meet with sudden disaster. A few yards up the lane, a horse regards us with his lovely, soft eyes. He is easily

The Colonel with his bodyguard.

captured by the private who mounts him, but when the colonel is ready for the road, he orders him to dismount and gets astride himself. We follow him on his charger and are greatly amused at his air of importance which he adopts for the occasion, gravely acknowledging salutes of imaginary troops. For a second, we halt, whilst the camera records a picture of the group. After riding a short way, the colonel slides gracefully to the ground and we proceed on our way. We now enter a little wood of tall pines close by the side of the Swale and on the lawn-like sward we fling off our packs. The dixie is filled with water and the sergeant-major lights a fire of pine twigs, the dixie resting across two stones. A farmhouse up the hill supplies us with eggs and a piece of fat 'tiger' which provides us with dripping in which to fry the eggs. It is here that the army has a laugh at the expense of the adjutant. Taking hold of one of the eggs he says, "Have any of you seen this done?" He then sends the egg spinning up in the air; it comes down a dozen paces away where it smashes as we expected it would. In vain the juggler tells us that it is possible to throw an egg in a field without its breaking, providing it does not strike some hard substance. We ridicule his assertion, refusing to believe in the egg-throwing creed. He tosses no more eggs that day, but vows that when eggs are again two for 1½d* he will treat us to an ocular demonstration. Our fire was making an abundance of smoke which curled over the dixie. To prevent the water from being smoked, the sergeant-major flings into it a piece of twig. This sounds like witchcraft, but it was effective and the water remained untainted. The eggs are sizzling in the dixie lid and as the water is about to boil, a handful of tea is thrown into the pan. The difficulty of plates is easily overcome and we revert to the primitive, utilising smooth clean stones on which we place the eggs. Thus washing up is easily accomplished by pitching our plates into the river! Sandwiches, sweets and pineapple chunks, as dessert, complete our repast. The site of our camp is ideal. Each side of the bank slopes easily down to the edge of the water and part of the river-bed seems to have been cobbled. We think that the place has been used as a ford. In the background is a rounded portion of a hill thickly covered with pine and larch. At the base of this, the river makes a graceful curve and then comes laughingly towards us, its bank fringed with overhanging greenery and its course well defined with beds of whitened pebbles. Across the river, a field or two distant, a passing cyclist denotes the position of the main road. The last egg is fried and eaten; we wash and after a short rest we are off again.

The sky is overcast and someone predicts rain. We cross the river by a substantial stone bridge and regain the main road which ascends rapidly for the next mile or so, but we get a grand view of the valley. Passing through a little place called Low Row we swing along to the tune of 'The Military Band'. Here we meet an old man with a pony and a light cart.

"There, that's grand!" he exclaims. "A bit of real, lively music." We tell him we are glad he has enjoyed it; perhaps he would like a hymn, we suggest? He declared that nothing would give him greater pleasure. We begin with 'Rock-a-bye baby'. . . . or rather, 'Beautiful Zion' and this is followed by several verses of 'Rimington'. He does not sing but listens intently, his face radiant with emotion. He is nearly blind but it is his face which portrays his inner feelings. His nearly sightless eyes are continually moving round and round, poignantly devoid of expression. We are a little group in the road; above us, on rising ground, is the 'Blue Bell Inn'. The landlady and her daughter emerge at the first strains of music. Nearby,

---

*In present-day decimal currency, 12 for 3.75p.!

several men are slating a roof but they stop their tapping to listen. Then an elderly man comes across to us and takes his place with the tenors.

Luckily he did, for our leading tenor nearly chokes owing to a midge becoming entangled in his epiglottis. Our old friend is lavish in his praise for he has enjoyed it very much. He thanks us and we leave him and his little Galloway to their work. Down the road we ask a little girl the distance to Reeth. "Two miles and a half," she answers. We walk nearly two miles and again we enquire of an old man, "How many miles to Reeth, please?" "Two and a half," he replies.

A shower of rain come on. We enter a field and creep into our capes, lying down until the rain ceases then, folding our 'tents' like Arabs, we gently steal away. A mile further on we ask a passing carter the mileage to Reeth. "A good three miles!" he assures us. Fair Reeth, thou elusive one, thou ever receding! In the shelter of a barn we put on our water-proofs, for the rain is now coming down in earnest. A drink at a well, "Wodzyours?" then "Forward, the hump brigade!" On our right is the boldly-defined Harkerside Moor and through the rain ahead, a dip in the hills is seen where runs the Arkle Beck. A welcome sight! Reeth now comes into our ken. The rain ceases as we enter the village, but with dripping capes and 'humps' we present rather a sorry spectacle. Our first endeavour was to find

Low Row.

lodgings but no-one seemed specially anxious to accommodate us. We try temperance hotels, other boarding establishments, inns, the 'Black Bull', the 'Red Lion' and the 'Pink Lion with Green Whiskers'! All are full of visitors. We contemplate asking for the proverbial clothes line, but after further enquiries, fortune again favours us and we eventually arrive at Arkle Mill House, where, Mrs. H. gives us a welcome. If you ever make Reeth your place of holiday stay, if possible, at Arkle Mill House which is pleasantly situated by the side of the Arkle Beck. If you like plenty of air space in your sleeping apartment, ask for the large bedroom. We get it; six of us in four beds with room for more! Lofty and spacious it is and we were to sleep well. Before tea, we bathe and change into dry clothes, then stroll into the large dining-room where we enjoy a good meal. We have a little music, then repair to the village green where we indulge in a game of cricket, using a tennis-racket for a bat. Owing to the rain, the 'match was abandoned'. We return to billets and for the rest of the evening Arkle House resounds to the strain of song and chorus.

Oh yes! We have an audience; several old ladies, friends of Mrs. H. also several young ladies of course, with hair bobbed after the manner of the Ancient Egyptians; Mr. H. and a young gentleman and his sister from Sunderland; Hilda, a vivacious girl of ten and round-eyed little William with his Wesleyan Methodist Missionary Box! Whilst supper is being prepared, we again visit the green to sing hymns. The night is lovely after the rain; the air is calm and the singing carries well. All round the green stand our listeners who show their appreciation by filling William's missionary box to overflowing. We slowly return at dusk to the house by Arkle Beck singing:

'Softly the shadows of the night round are falling,
Wearily homeward we"re wending our way,
Toil with the light and repose with the night,
Peace comes with rest at the close of the day.'

Reeth is built on the hillside at the entrance to Arkengarthdale about a mile above the confluence of the Arkle Beck with the Swale. It is a picturesque village, neat cottages and quaint hostelries surround the spacious village green with its may-pole and old-time stocks. There is an attractiveness about the place which pleases us and year by year it is gaining in popularity as a place for a holiday.

DAY FOUR . . . TUESDAY

REETH TO RICHMOND

O ur bill paid, we leave Arkle House and saunter down the village. The maiden ladies at the post-office thank us for our hymn singing. We are elated at their remarks and show our appreciation by buying some stamps! As we cross the river bridge we meet again our half-blind acquaintance of the previous day. We greet him with a cheery "Good morning!"

He muses, "Now where have I met you gentlemen before? I know! You are the people who sang for me yesterday and I thought what a noble work you were doing in singing as you did. Good morning gentlemen and thank you."

"Good morning, dad! You're welcome," we echo.

To our right we notice the Norman tower of the church at Grinton. We miss this little place as again we avoid the main road and proceed along the old coach road from Reeth to Richmond. This is a fine, breezy walk over the uplands from whence we obtain a splendid view of the valley of the Swale and the hilly North Riding. It is pleasant walking along this plateau of fell-land with its miles of undulating grit road in front of us. Miles ahead, a chimney-like object among a clump of trees claims our attention. It is a stone obelisk which is associated with some little piece of family history which at present we forget. This morning we are all in excellent spirits. Feelings ride high as the cloud, wit and humour flow freely. We march along to the tunes of well-known airs, whistled and sung and now we descend into the Vale of Marske singing 'The Ash Grove' — 'Down yonder green valley where streamlets meander'. This hamlet of Marske is beautifully situated in a well-wooded valley through which runs the Marske Beck, a tributary of the Swale. We leave Marske, after lunch at the Temperance Hotel, our army reinforced by an Irish colleen — a sports girl who accompanies us to Richmond. She is put into the care of the corporal who keeps the conversation wagging. To prevent a repetition of the inglenook episode, the private is detailed off to look for mushrooms. In his quest he ranges the hillside and successfully finds some good specimens of edible fungi. In the good old days, highwaymen on these roads demanded, "Money or your life!" Today, a mounted man stops us to ask for a cigarette! We follow a rather reddish grit road which winds up the hill by an ancient lime-kiln. Again the view is worthy of the climb. The hills of Swaledale stand out boldly and well-defined but as we proceed their altitude diminishes until, at last, they finally merge into a well-wooded plain beyond Richmond. Across the low-lying hills is the white road which leads into Wensleydale, beyond which the long flat summit of Penhill stands out conspicuously. There are several landmarks on our left; an area of tree stumps scarred and blackened by fire reminds us of some of the battle-scarred regions of France and Flanders. Further on is a relic of the Napoleonic Wars, a beacon, a basket-like arrangement of iron hoops on a pedestal. Lastly we pass the grandstand of Richmond race course. A long, straight road leads us down into the mediaeval town of Richmond with its quaint market place and adjacent hostelries, its ancient castle and priory.

Market Place, Richmond

Richmond Market Place.

29

Richmond from the Terrace.

In the narrow thoroughfare we part company with Patsy, the Irish girl. Later, she will return to Marske by the newer, main road. We now wander round the town in search of lodgings and eventually fortune (or misfortune) brings us to the 'House of Mystery'. The bell pull being out of order, we knock at the door. . .once. . . .twice. . .three times. Then the door opened quietly and the hard-featured 'Madame Tussaud' confronted us. As she listens to our enquiry, she eyes us over severely before bidding us enter. In frigid tones she asks, "Who sent you here? Where have you come from? Where are you going and what are you prepared to pay?"

We answer her questions and assure her of our solvency, telling her to present her bill next morning when she shall receive prompt settlement. She tells us that she never takes in one-night visitors; all her guests come for long periods — oh, two or three months at a time! As a rule they enjoy themselves so much that it is with great reluctance that they leave her hospitable roof for the comforts of their own homes. She places a forefinger on her lips and thoughtfully regards the faded carpet for a moment. She then leaves the room to confer with her sister who, by the way, we never see. We are not favourably impressed by the place and suggest a retreat but our remarks are cut short by the reappearance of madam who, after more meditating, condescends to take us in. We tactfully observe that perhaps we are putting her to too much trouble; but no, we are very welcome to stay and she will do her best to make us comfortable. Stoically we accept the inevitable and decide to stay. We are next shown to a bedroom, scantily furnished with a rickety wash-stand and a massive set of drawers with a wardrobe at each end. The floor was covered with a drab oilcloth from which the pattern had long since vanished, with a piece of frayed carpet by the side of the washstand. In one corner stood a hard-looking bed on which three of us slept that night. We had warm water brought to us in an enamelled jug which was badly blackened by soot, it having been used to heat the water it contained. After making arrangements for a hot dinner with stewed mushrooms to flavour, we again saunter out into the sunlight. In the market-place we meet Mrs. P. who is sister to Mrs. H. of Muker. She gives us an invitation to spend the evening at her home. They have a good piano and are very fond of music. We accept her hospitality and later give them a little concert.

It is a pleasant stroll around the castle walls, along the path known as 'Castle Walk'. Here the cliff rises steeply from the river and massive buttresses have their foundation upon the solid rock. Truly, our lusty fore-fathers had nothing more to learn about the building of walls! From this terrace the view is excellent and through the trees we observe the river below. We hear the sound of water falling over a weir, then the river flows peacefully onwards to the plain beyond. There is a fine old bridge over the river, while underneath the very shadow of the mighty castle walls huddle the red-tiled houses of old Richmond. There is no uniformity about these clustered dwellings.

This is obvious at once to those accustomed to seeing row after row of houses identical with one another. We get a delightful study of angles of chimney stacks and gables, and the effect of light and shade is most remarkable. We are reminded that during the feudal period the site of these dwellings would be occupied by the huts and hovels of my lord"s serfs, who cringed before him when he passed with his retinue of steel-clad followers. The old Keep (twelfth century) is recognised as one of the finest of our Norman fortresses. In front of the Keep is an ancient Russian cannon which was a trophy of the Crimean War. With its spiked touch-hole, it is now useless.

Having completed the circuit of the castle, we return to the apartments of madam and after a reasonably good dinner we quickly clear out and make for the neat, little parlour of Mrs. P. opposite the old priory. On leaving here at 9.30 p.m. we make a detour to arrive at the 'House of Mystery' punctually at ten o'clock. Madam is awaiting our return and has two candles already lit. Straightaway she takes us to our rooms and gingerly we follow in her wake up the creaking stairway which is full of flitting shadows. As arranged, the adjutant, corporal and private occupy one bedroom and these three bid fare-well to their comrades who now follow madam up another flight of stairs. There is something uncanny in the oppressive silence of this house which we cannot explain and, strange to say, we are all affected by the same feeling. The corporal, usually the most merry of company, now begins to talk about murders and ghosts and warns us to have our 'revolvers and toothpicks' ready in case of emergency. Just before sleep claims us there is a tapping on the floor above, followed by a thud.

"They're knocking for help," whispers the corporal. "there, that's one of them done for! They'll be coming down here next," he woefully concludes. But nothing further happens and presently we doze off to sleep.

DAY FIVE . . . WEDNESDAY

RICHMOND TO LEYBURN

After the alarms and uncertainties of the previous night, we need little persuasion to get ready for the road, and after breakfast we sally forth into the old town. Winding our way through narrow, cobbled streets, we cross the river bridge and ascend the hill, turning for another glimpse of the place where, once upon a time, 'there lived a lass more bright than May-Day morn', immortalised in the old ballad 'The Lass of Richmond Hill'. It is good to be alive this jolly morning in July and for walking the conditions are ideal. We have a fine tramp before us. A fresh breeze blows across our path, clouds float high and fleeing shadows give way to frequent bursts of sunshine. The road runs between well-trimmed hedgerows bright with blossoms. On each side a strip of grass is bejewelled with flowers. The song of birds and the dreamy hum of passing insects create a joyful medley of sounds. Now a timid rabbit scampers up the road to find a burrow in a thicket of dogwood. For miles, the road ascends the hill at an easy gradient; fields and meadows are left behind, now moor and heathland dominate; hedges give way to walls and wire fencing whilst heath plants such as bird's-foot trefoil, bedstraw and wild thyme are in profusion. Reaching the summit of the hill we lie down on the turf while the sweet moorland air plays about us. In contrast, we think of the people we know holiday-making among the giddy throng at crowded seaside resorts, but we do not envy them. No, we would not "swap"! Looking back, we observe Richmond with its ancient fortress still visible. Away to the right there is the silver gleam of distant water on the plain, whilst we also see the entrance to the Vale of Marske and the range of hills we traversed yesterday. "Oh, hills and dales, we leave you with regret but with many happy memories. Goodbye, Swaledale! Come on, lads!"

We are now walking over a breezy common open to the moor which falls away to our right, a world of ling and heather, in a depression which rises again to meet a distant hill. Down the sandy, grit road we meet a fellow

Leyburn Market Square.

hiker with his ruck-sack. We greet him cheerily and pass on. From a farmyard which is full of sheep and lambs there comes a pitiful bleating. Several farmers are busily engaged shearing the sheep and for a few minutes we stop to view this animated scene. A sheep is caught, there is a short struggle and the sheep is on its back between the sturdy legs of the farmer who soon gets busy with the shears. A few minutes suffice to remove the fleece which is now tied into a bundle by the farm lad who then throws it through the doorway of a loft, where three or four red-faced youngsters eagerly await its coming. The shorn sheep is next branded with the owner's initials or some other distinguishing mark, hot tar being used for this purpose. Then a sheepdog finally chases the creature to the crowd of bleaters in another part of the yard. At a nearby well, we slake our thirst. "Now then, major, wodjergointoave?" This is the first drink we have had since leaving Richmond and we enjoy it greatly. Further on we meet two young ladies who ask the way to Richmond. Turning, we point out the sandy road which winds down from the moor we have just crossed. These young ladies, like us, are on a walking tour and earlier in the week have just come down Wensleydale. We tell them that we have been to Hawes and they then ask us if we visited Hell Ghyll, but we reply in the negative. After a few more words about road maps and the weather, we wish them good afternoon. Out of earshot, we again mention Hell Ghyll. "Oh, that's it!" said one. "I missed the final word in that sentence and was feeling a trifle uncomfortable!" He then kicks an old straw hat into the hedge. "By jove, I'm ready for dinner." So are we all and it is a hungry half-dozen who enter the little village of Bellerby half an hour later. A greybeard is removing some old hay to make room for a new stack so we ask him if he can recommend a place of refreshment. He directs us to the 'Cross Keys' as the most likely place to get something to eat, so thither we go. A healthy looking young woman asks our requirements but she is sorry that she is unable to provide a hot meal. Bread and cheese is the best she can do. We are ravenous and request that she bring out the victuals, slabs of real Wensleydale and good home-made bread. This we wash down with mineral water and enjoy a real good feed. Our throats moistened we feel like singing and warble several of our favourites. Through the window, we perceive several youngsters who are attracted to the scene by the sound of music. One of them, a most comical little chap, is pretending to beat time and it is with difficulty that we can refrain from laughing outright. Just as we are leaving the inn an elderly lady asks us to sing another song. We oblige with, "Oh who will o'er the Downs?" which pleases her immensely. Then a tall young fellow comes to the door and says, "Now, boys, won't you have a drink with me?" We refuse him gently but firmly, with thanks, telling him that we have just supped. A shade of disappointment passes over his face as we move off. We are followed by the small boys of the village. The sergeant-major has a postcard he wishes to despatch and the comical boy volunteers to take it to the post-office. For this service he demands one cigarette as payment. He then goes on his errand with a bodyguard of younger boys. the happiest lad in Bellerby. We can imagine how he would later light his 'fag' with great deliberation and manly air, behind some barn. How he would be the centre of an admiring but envious crowd of 'mere kids' as he would think them. Perhaps he might conde-scend to let one or two of the more favoured have a 'draw', but the rest would have to be content with watching the operation. After a pleasant walk of about one hour, we reach Leyburn, a clean healthy place with a wide space instead of the usual village green. All the buildings are of a most substantial character. We like the place and decide to stay the night. At the second attempt, we secure apartments at the 'Golden Lion' hotel. Here we have excellent accommodation, good beds, splendid fare and civility from all.

After a meal we call on Mr. William Horne, F.G.S., clockmaker and antiquary, but his son, Mr. John Horne, informs us that his father is not at home, having gone away with two friends that very morning. The combined age of these three gentlemen is 250 years, surely proof of the healthiness of Leyburn. With great courtesy, John Horne shows us his father's collection of antiquities which, be it noted, is one of the finest private museums in the country. Mr Horne illustrates to us the use of the tinder-box and the art of making fire by this primitive method. There is a funnel-shaped pen of copper which was once used in the mulling of ale. Here are several quaint ale measures of pewter and one of glass which is specially interesting since it is a yard long. These ale-sticks would be placed in conspicuous positions in old taverns and the unwary would often fall into the trap. A 'yard of ale' would be given to anyone who drank it from the measure without removing his lips during the ceremony. At first the liquid would flow but gradually a vacuum formed in the wider end of the glass until suction made further drinking impossible. Finally, the drinker on removing his mouth, allowed the air to rush in and he received the remaining contents full in the face, much to the delight of the company present.

In another corner of the room are about a dozen beautiful paintings of wild flowers. These are executed on vellum and are perfect in colour and detail. Even when viewed through a magnifying glass we fail to detect a flaw. Of these, John Ruskin, the great art critic, said, "Few can equal and none can excel." Among the numerous curiosities which claimed our attention were moulds for leaden spoons, the dog catcher, and an article of similar pattern which a stout old lady once used to lift small objects from the floor. Then there was a cavalier"s boot, old weapons, flint instruments, Pharaoh's bowl (a gift from Professor Petrie), John Wesley's seal, a 'leather bottel', geological specimens, polished stones, etc., and lastly the visitor's book in which we inscribed our names. After thanking Mr. Horne for his kindness, we leave his genial company and next visit the church which stands at the lower end of the village. Later, we have an excellent dinner at the 'Golden Lion', followed by a rest and a smoke.

In the evening we walk along what is known as 'Leyburn Shawl', a path running along the edge of a limestone cliff which is parallel to the valley. Its sides are covered with trees and shrubbery, a pleasant walk; two miles of gradually ascending path. What a glorious view of the valley! Most prominent of all is Penhill Beacon. Tonight its bracken covered slopes are illumined with the golden glow of the setting sun, and even when shadows have crept across the vale and distant hills show blue, its long summit still reflects the glory of the departing day. A cool, clean breeze blows upon us. We pass a place called 'Queen's Gap' and on our next jaunt we shall have to make further mention of this sylvan glade. Then we retrace our steps through fields where rabbits feed among the brackens and dewy grasses. Vain are the efforts of the private to make a capture, and once in his mad chasing he came near to falling headlong over the cliff. Well! Our hotel at last and a pleasant sleep at the end of a most enjoyable day.

DAY SIX . . . THURSDAY

LEYBURN TO WEST BURTON

We are in good form at the beginning of this, our sixth day's tramp. For some unaccountable reason, the sergeant-major disappears and keeps the company waiting for quite some time, whereupon there is much grumbling in the ranks. Now if it had been the private, there would have been a row! The sergeant-major returns and we quietly move away. We follow the main road by the Shawl Woods to Preston-under-Scar and then to Wensley, the most picturesque village in the Dale. Under a large sycamore we sing two hymns and we have several listeners. It is recorded that John Wesley preached on this village green under a tree, perhaps the same tree that now protects us from the hot sun. Being pedestrians, we are allowed to walk through Bolton Park which is the

Wensley, Bolton Hall.

shorter way to Redmire. Passing through the lodge gates, we traverse a long avenue of stately trees and feast our eyes on the broad acres of rich pastures on which fine cattle are quietly browsing. We enter the woods where there are many fine specimens of forest trees and although the sun is at its most powerful, we walk in comparative gloom. There is a strong scent of woodland plants. Here we find enchanter's nightshade, sweet woodruff and wood sanicle, while from among the carpet of dog's mercury leaves there rears the taller burdock, marsh angelica and giant hogweed. Further on are sombre clumps of firs and pines with drifts of brown needles about their trunks. But the flies are still troublesome and we again resort to the protection of the handkerchief! In one place there is a vista almost equal to the famous 'Surprise View' of Studley at Fountains Abbey, with a break in the foliage and a straight reach of shimmering river between leafy banks. We pass Bolton Hall, the beautiful residence of Lord Bolton, a fine, substantial building in a natural garden. Finally, we come to the edge of the wood where a strange antediluvian creature guards the gateway. This is a fallen tree of peculiar animal form in which someone has fixed a glass eye!

Now along a narrow country lane and we obtain a view of Redmire and that noble pile of ruins, Bolton Castle. Where a stream floods the lane, we meet a gentlemen coming leisurely along. We give him a cheery greeting whereupon he stops and we engage in converstion. He is from Whitby, down here on holiday; a man of education we imagine from his speech. He is most interested in our wanderings and our mode of travel. Whilst staying in Switzerland (pre-war) he said, Germans were everywhere with their familiar ruck-sacks. He would like to see this method of holiday-making more copied in our own country. A farmer with a horse and cart now goes splashing along the flooded roadway. Our newly-made acquaintance turns and walks with us to the little limestone village of Redmire, a delightful place of abode. During a few minutes halt, we make the welkin ring with, 'Oh, who will o'er the Downs?' our friend joining in the last verse with a fine bass voice. He then escorts us to the lane which leads directly to the castle. We walk round the ancient walls and up a flight of steps leading to a massive door. A typical Daleswoman invites us in and asks if we require something to eat. We reply in the affirmative and whilst dinner is being prepared we visit the museum which is most educative and interesting. The articles which mostly appealed to our imagination are an iron-bound Spanish Armada treasure chest and relics of the Middle Ages, other exhibits being too numerous to mention. Then we climb up spiral staircases and wander through echoing chambers, the sleeping apartments, dining hall, and 'Mary, Queen of Scots room' where, it is said, the royal captive was imprisoned, but from where she subsequently escaped. The following description of the affair from Halliwell Sutcliffe's 'By Moor and Fen' is worthy of repetition.

'And it was then that Mary, Queen of Scots, was brought a prisoner to Bolton Castle, a prisoner because Elizabeth suspected her of being a traitor to the realm, and because Elizabeth was sure that her rival possessed a fairer face and sweeter manner than herself . . . It was setting spark to tinder to bring the hapless Stuart Queen so near to the Norton menfolk. Her cause lacked no single quality that was calculated to appeal to their reckless, large-hearted sense of chivalry. Her beauty, her wit, her tender grace, were well-known to all men by repute; to these, now that she was in the hands of jealous foes were added helplessness and that suggestion of suffering which gives a new persuasiveness to beauty. Small wonder that Mary was scarce housed in Bolton Castle before Christopher Norton was up and across the fells, with a vow that before the moon was old, he would pluck the Scottish Queen from her prison . . .

He rode boldly up to the gates of the castle, our hot knight errant, secured admission under pretext of loyalty to Elizabeth and was given the post of one of the guard in immediate attendance upon the Queen of Scots. He made summer-love to the Queen's ladies and played the peacock for Lord Scrope's benefit and hoodwinked the good man completely. The lad's courage was indomitable; after biding his time with what patience he could muster, he contrived to bring a led-horse under Mary's window, her favourite maid on honour helped to lower her by a rope, and in the sequel young Norton succeeded in getting clear away into the woods with the royal captive.

The local gentry were all for Mary — as good Yorkshiremen were like to be with their love of beauty and fair play — and a party of these were waiting at the edge of the woods when Christopher Norton reached it with his royal companion. The garrison of Bolton

Castle, however, had taken the alarm by this time and had turned out pell- mell in pursuit. Their horses were the better and they overtook Norton and those with him at an open forest glade thereafter known as Queen's Gap, and fought a bloody fray there, two to one, and carried Mary back in triumph to the castle."

Before we proceed further, we notice with regret that so many members of the 'Disfigurement Society' have found their way into this historic pile. These persons have literally covered the walls in some of the chambers with their initials, scratched and written. In fact, we should imagine that one room was used as their headquarters at one time, for there seems to be as much blacklead as whitewash on the walls. A notice politely asks visitors not to write on the walls, but the 'initialist' takes no heed of notices. If he can find a square inch of whitewash, a smooth piece of woodwork or a pane of glass, deftly he will write or scratch his name, then after contemplating his handiwork, he goes away well satisfied. Why anyone should take the trouble to write his name fourteen feet above the floor, we cannot say. It is a psychological problem!

We are amply repaid for our climb to the leads, for the day is very clear and the view we obtain from these lofty battlements is superb. From the woods and trees come the ceaseless twitterings of feathered songsters and a congregation of starlings rise, turn, and fall again in wonderful precision. Hamlets and farms come under our gaze and a distant wisp of vapour from the railway engine reminds us that we are living in the age of steam. Then the hills; most prominent of all is Penhill, further back the rounded, heather-clad grit moors and crossing the valley again, the lofty limestone fells of Wensleydale. Rovingly, our eyes survey the beauty of this panorama of hills and the scenery of this delightful dale.

We wind our way down the narrow stairs and find dinner ready for us in a quaint, little parlour. The light comes through the leaded panes of a window set in five feet thick wall, where there is a cosy window seat from which there is a grand view. The meal proceeds and Mrs. S. is kept busy feeding six old-time knights whom we now try to ape.

Sir Bedivere: "Dost see a glint o'weapons ahint yon wood, Lancelot?"

Sir Lancelot: "Tis but the sunlight on the river that thou seest old scarebones. Methinks, that since that last foray, thy nerves have been highly strung, for thou canst see a Highland bonnet behind every bush and a spear in every glitter o'water."

41

Sir Marmaduke: "Blame not his nerves, Lancelot, bur rather the skinfuls of sour ale that his is wont to drink."

Sir Bedivere: "By my jerkin! You speak lightly o'my fears, but ye southerners know little o'swift invasion and the Scots will descend again, say I."

Sir Lancelot: "Granted the 'Barelegs' do come again, we must be wary, but there is nothing to be gained by getting up the wind'. My motto is, 'let us eat, drink and be merry' for tomorrow we don't walk far, and a blight on the Scots!"

Sir Bedivere: "Wilt pass hither the marmalade, Sir Marmaduke?"

Whilst this scene is being enacted, the junior major is busy scribbling and the following are his lines on Bolton Castle, written at the dinner table:

'Thou towering crest, erect upon the hillside,
That frownest down the peaceful, quiet vale,
Open out thy secret past, and tell me,
Sojourning here, I fain would hear they tale.
Tell me tales of long since departed,
Of love and romance and the thrilling fight.
Of laughter ringing thro' thy heavy arches,
Of wailing in the endless, cheerless night.
Tell me of maid upon yon moss-grown turret,
Waving her lover speedily gaily forth.
Tell me of woman, sick at heart and weary,
Waiting — dreading the chill tale of death.
A story tell of some long-forgotten feud,
When air was pregnant with unending strife,
And blows fell hard and red blood flowing,
Stirring the hour with keener zest for life.
What canst thou tell of the ill-fated Mary?
Poor victim of another's hateful spleen.
Heard'st not the prayer for consolation
That rant the knell of what might have been.
What mock and sham of priest and creed observing,
Thy cynic walls have gathered in their span.
And yet hath noted in uncut jewels dwelling
The undimmed spark divine in everyman.
Thus thy tale would carry back the memory

42

To that past which holds such golden store,
And by its tale of cruelty and failings
Bids us live, still higher than before.
Adieu, ye walls, and thanks I gladly render
For thy great past and the lessons thou hast taught.
More joyful, I upon my way shall wander,
Knowing the highest, the more dearly bought.'

After dinner we happen to mention to Mrs. S. that it is just six years since last we were here. Tears well up in the good woman's eyes when she says that much has happened since then. She shows us a photograph of a fine lad in uniform, her son. It is the old tale, far too common, of a youth who went to war, but never returned. One of the brave who met Fate or Destiny on the battlefields of France and, we'll warrant, one of a long line of menfolk who left this historic castle to fight for creed or king. On the wall hangs an old flintlock shotgun, a finely made, beautifully finished weapon which, if it could speak, could tell some stirring tales of poaching forays It is an heirloom and belonged to Mr. S'. grandfather. Mrs. S. now relates its history.

"Grandfather S. was a gamekeeper who once walked in fear of his life, having had trouble with some poachers. They had sworn to kill him.

One day, as he was walking down a lane, he was suddenly confronted by two men, one with a gun already at his shoulder. He gave himself up for lost, but rushed upon the men. The trigger was pulled, the gun misfired, and the would-be murders took to their heels, leaving the gun on the ground. That is how the weapon came into the family's possession and Lord Bolton himself could not purchase it."

In another little parlour there is a harmonium and a Wesleyan Methodist tune book. At Mrs. S'. request we render several of our favourite tunes. Then she shows us parts of the building that are being repaired. Here the Norman masonry has been marvellously copied by the modern builder engaged on the work. One of the towers is being repaired and possibly the chapel will be roofed again. But these reconstructions will mean a heavy bill for Lord Bolton who, we are told, is very enthusiastic of the work in hand.

"On the 4th day of July, 1379, Richard le Scrope, afterwards Chancellor of England and Warden of the Western Marches, obtained royal licence to castellate his manor house of Bolton, which he completed during the reign of Richard II at an expense of £12,000 — in those days an enormous sum. The timber was chiefly brought from Inglewood Forest in Cumberland by divers draughts of oxen and the stone appears to have been taken from the adjacent quarry. Bolton Castle was gallantly defended in the time of Charles I against the Parliamentary forces and Colonel Chaynor held it until the garrison was reduced to eating horse flesh. He capitulated on the 5th day of November, 1645, and marched for Pontefract. In 1647, the Committee of York ordered the castle to be rendered untenable."

There is something about the old place which immediately takes us back to the days 'when knights were bold and barons held their sway'. Its old halls and crumbling walls still breathe the spirit of romance. In imagination, we can see the knights in their armour, the men-at-arms with leather jerkins and gauntlets, archers carrying the good yew bows and crossbow men with their cumbersome but more deadly weapons. Trained at the village butts, these English bowmen came second to none in their archery. Then there is the spectacle of the tournament when the knight tried his best to spit his opponent on his lance; all this playfulness in honour of my lady's fair face! Next, the hunt and the bringing home of the venison, all-night carousals, Christmas festivities and the festive board. So we could go on if we had the time, but we must be away. On our departure, Mrs. S. stands on the lofty steps and waves her goodbye. Then we amble through the fields and reach the main road. On this road we meet an artist with his stool and sketching materials. He bids us a 'Good afternoon, glorious weather! Shortly afterwards, we leave the road and follow a cart track through fields of waving, rustling oats. Their green panicles gracefully bend and whisper secrets to each other, secrets which the yellow mustard must not hear, although its golden bloom enlivens half the field.

Our track leads us to a farmhouse. In the yard there is a capstan-like wheel, about a foot from the ground, and this is geared to a shaft which runs into the barn where it is connected to the threshing machine. Two or more horses are harnessed to the long arms of the capstan and then the animals are driven round and round. Over a stile, we continue our walk through the fields and at a gate a number of young bullocks grudgingly make way for us. Presently we come into an old, winding lane bordered with a profusion of meadow geranium whose opal tints are exquisite. Over the wall, several men are busy with the hoe but find time to watch us pass. On our right we observe the village of Carperby but our route is not in that direction. We soon reach the highway again and proceed in the direction of Aysgarth, marching to the songs we enjoy. Two miles along this road brings us within sound of the River Ure and we decide to visit the famous falls. To the left, a notice indicates the way, over a stile and along winding paths amid park-like scenery, clumps of alder and hazel with swelling filberts. We follow a blind path which leads us into the scrub by the side of the river. Instead of retracing our steps, we push on through thickets of bramble and overhanging branches, through squelching mosses and beds of equisetum, where there is a strong smell of whorled mint. Twisting and turning in Indian file, we follow imaginary paths until finally we emerge onto a shelf of limestone sloping down to the swirling river. We easily make our way over these rocks which display all the vestiges of life of a byegone age. With the river becoming more turbulent as we advance, we soon reach the place where the whole river rushes over the rocks in a seething cauldron. Beyond the range of disturbed water there is a pool of inky blackness, with masses of foam floating like ducks on the surface. These eddy slowly round under the overhanging rocks and later merrily join the rapidly moving river below the pool. The weather is glorious. The sunlight plays on the rushing foam-flecked cataract and the noise of the falling waters drowns our feeble voices.

Aysgarth Bridge and Upper Fall.

We sit on a ledge of rock and contemplate the grandeur of the scene. As we have said before, there is a strange fascination about a waterfall and a charm which cannot be described. Aysgarth Falls rank high amongst the finest in England and, for summer-time, we imagine we now see them at their best, the heavy rains of the previous weeks having filled the head-springs to overflowing. Our packs adjusted, we take a last look round and climb the path which leads us through the bushes to the natural park above. Had we time, we would linger here a while to describe this garden of nature, but it would be folly to attempt a word picture when Turner himself has put its charms on canvas. On the road once more, we reach the Ure again, with the old mill grinding out its precious dust. Above, on a lofty eminence stands Aysgarth Church, a stately edifice of Gothic architecture. We cross the Ure by a handsome bridge and view the Upper Falls which are tumbling grandly.

"Here's a well, corporal! Wodjergointohave? Wodz yours, sergeant-major?"

"After you with the drinking cup, lance-corporal." For it must be mentioned that our private was promoted at Bolton Castle.

We cannot enter the church which is kept locked on account of a case of vandalism which occurred some time ago. We pass through the church-yard and a few minutes' walk through the fields brings us to the attractive little village of Aysgarth itself. We have happy recollections of a previous stay. The post office is now besieged for 'Poste Restante' letters and postcards promised us by other fellows' sisters now on holiday somewhere near Keswick. Our correspondence read, we walk along the road as far as the vicarage, then proceed through the fields on our right and over the hill towards West Burton. Before descending into the valley, we take a farewell look at the dale we are leaving. Eight days is but a short time in which to view even the most interesting of places. Eight weeks or, better still, eight years would be more to the mark. We are sorry that our itinerary does not include such places as West Witton, historic Middleham, romantic Askrigg or quaint little Bainbridge, where the old hornblower once made the village echo to his blasts. All around us are the fells which we have encircled on our travels. Away in the distance we espy Bolton Castle and now Penhill has changed its profile and we hardly recognise it. "Well, au revoir, sweet vale! May your cheeses never grow stale!" Over the brow of the hill, the prospect is alluring. Facing us are rugged limestone fells, a narrow valley

West Burton.

and a singing brook which rushes down from its cradle on the bleak moorlands. Up the dale the roofs of West Burton come into view. We wend our way down the hillside which is tinged in places with the red of wood betony. In a little dell, the numerous, flowerless stalks of the wild hyacinth remind us of a departed tint of colour which must have been on this same hillside in springtime. But then, 'every dog has his day and every flower its season'.

We cross the beck by a narrow footbridge and reach the main road which we follow up the valley to West Burton where we hope to find food and lodging. We enter this clean, old village at about six o'clock. The party is gathered by the market cross, laughing at the junior major who is sitting with his feet protruding through the village stocks. The adjutant and sergeant-major — again the most presentable — bustle around in search of 'digs'. Mrs. S., whose house we have had recommended, is unable to accommodate us. The 'Black Bull' declines to supply us with tea, milk or bed. (Fancy going to a 'Black Bull' for milk!) They again cross the green, their progress followed by four pairs of anxious eyes. Two more houses are tried in vain. Then an old woman, with a basket of eggs, directs them to the cottage of Mrs. J. on the opposite side of the sward. This time, something must be done, for the hunger of the army is great and we are resolved to stay the night in the village. As the billet-hunters again pass the four hungry-looking individuals by the stocks, the colonel gives them injunctions to 'look slippy' and to 'get a move on'. Mrs. J. is sorry, she had no food to spare and on that account cannot take us in. But, stay! Something in the speech or bearing of her would-be guests tells her that we are not common tramps. (What vanity!). The sergeant-major goes to interview the landlady of the 'Fox & Hounds' leaving the adjutant conversing with Mrs. J. and her daughter. The sergeant-major returns with a satisfied smile on his face. He reports, "The inn can give us food but no beds." For the fourth time the adjutant and the daughter exchange smiles and after assuring us that something will be done, she and her mother retire and hold a hurried consultation. A neighbour now comes to the rescue with two more beds, and these motherly women agree that we can stay for the night. At a signal, the four figures by the cross come eagerly to the billets, a huge smile on every face. At the stated time, we make our way across to the cosy parlour of the little inn where a good meal, beautifully served, is awaiting us. Never did tea seem so refreshing, never were wholesome victuals more acceptable and never, we should think, have six more hungry ramblers sat at the table in this old hostelry. The private — we beg his pardon — the lance-corporal was the first to finish, but his appetite revived at the appearance of more sustenance and, sad to relate, he continued eating, even unto the last!

Whilst we are resting, it would now be appropriate to say a few words about the village. Previously we have crowned Wensley as the most picturesque village in the valley of the Ure. We believe that the postal address of West Burton is Wensleydale. But it stands above the confluence of the Bishopdale Beck with the Walden Beck, the latter flowing close to the village, so we cannot be wrong when we say that it is in Bishopdale! On this point we must be clear, for now we unanimously vote West Burton the most outstanding village we have seen. It is grandly sheltered with the hills on three sides and on the fourth is a fine view of Wensleydale and the hills beyond. On rounding a corner the whole village springs into sight; two rows of detached and semi-detached dwellings smile at each other across the green which stretches the length of the village. The cottages are very clean and some of the older ones have ivy-covered walls. There are also a few modern houses with trim gardens in front. At the top of the green, the 'Black Bull' occupies a central position; at the lower end is the old smithy with several cartwheels and an old sledge propped against its walls. Further down still, a barn, a newly painted cart and a lot of hens! There is a market cross, the village stocks but lately restored and a maypole. The grocer's shop, which we patronise, has an excellent assortment of chocolates and a wide collection of postcards of local views. Facing the village green are seats on which several ladies are enjoying the salubrious atmosphere of this glorious summer evening. Now, five or six young fellows come onto the scene with a football and all, from the colonel downwards, soon join the leather kickers. From these young men we learn that football is by far the most popular game in this village and that cricket is very seldom played on the green. At the lower end of West Burton is a branch of the Wensleydale Dairy Company, built by the side of the Walden Beck. A little higher up the stream is a splendid waterfall called the Mill Fall. Having heard of the beauty of this sight, three of us have come to while away an hour or so. We cross a little stone bridge and find a seat on the left bank of the stream. We are immediately given a welcome by 'Ginger', the dairy cat, being the gentleman that he is. 'Ginger' springs onto our knees and walks around our necks, purring all the time. He is very frisky this evening; Lion-like, he crouches down and measures his distance to a piece of fox-tail grass. He springs upon it, turns a somersault and scurries out of sight. Presently, he reappears and goes through another series of antics for our benefit, for the more we laugh at him, the more entertaining he becomes. 'Ginger' is off duty, but believes in this exercise to keep himself fit, for the serious business of mouse catching is nerve-wracking to say the least — especially for the mouse!

Our attentions and exclamations now centre on a swarm of midges. They are most troublesome but experience has taught us that for every midge we kill, a dozen come to its funeral. The best remedy we find for dispersing them is tobacco smoke, and the lance-corporal, who never smokes, finally accepts a cigarette and does his bit like a man. We leave the frisking 'Ginger' and the midges and follow the bank of the stream to the overhanging rocks at the foot of the falls. Here, the peaty water rushes over its rocky ledge and falls with muffled roar into the dark pool at our feet. The sun's rays strike on the ascending spray producing a rainbow in miniature. Where the water flows from the pool, there is a narrow channel about a yard wide, a small scale Strid. This, the sergeant-major jumps, but his feet go too fast for his body and he falls flat on his back, fortunately

'Ginger', the dairy cat.

none the worse for this mishap. We return to the village green where some enthusiasts are still kicking a football whilst wearing their slippers! The sun is sinking behind the hills of Wensleydale, dew is forming on the grass and after our footballers finish their game a hush and quiet comes over all. The sun sets, its slanting rays hit upon moving clouds above the fells; twilight creeps upon us, the spirit of evening is approaching. We are a group on a seat; behind us our place of lodging with the homely Dales-women gossiping in the doorway. For the next hour or so, our voices are raised in song, hymn and chorus. Our repertoire is varied and includes all kinds of musical items. Whether the figures around the green enjoy it or not, we make no enquiry, but for our own part we have a thoroughly enjoyable time. In the little back kitchen, where we repair later, we are again requested to sing for an elderly lady who has come to listen to us. We oblige! The adjutant casually mentions that he was last in this village six years ago. "Were you on your honeymoon?" asks Mrs. J. The adjutant blushes and answers in the negative. Then he promptly turns the conversation to cheese-making and we discuss this most important industry of the Dales until bedtime. We retire to rest in three beds — a trio, a duo and a solo!

DAY SEVEN . . . FRIDAY

WEST BURTON TO PATELEY BRIDGE

The morning is dull and grey for rain has fallen during the night. Down the village, cows are lowing, a dog barks and a man shouts at the dog; cocks are crowing and hens are cackling. The lance-corporal is dressed and goes to waken the officers. In the 'Fox & Hounds' breakfast is on the table when we arrive and a goodly smell of 'tiger' and fried eggs assails our nostrils. All arrive in due course and the breakfast proceeds merrily. Our bill paid, we return to the cottages for our packs. So, once again, we are ready for the road and a stiff walk we have in front of us. Before leaving, Mrs. J. tells us that "when we get to t'top o' t'hill" we must be careful to turn to our left or else we shall come down into Walden again. We bear this in mind and with a parting verse of 'Rimington' we are of across the green and up the white road which leads us away from this charming retreat. We turn to our left and follow the steep fell road up the hill, giving our greetings to an elderly man who is cleaning out a ditch. We pass a ruined farmhouse and later cross the Walden Beck where we meet a farmer, his wife and two young ladies. They are in a gig and smile at us as we pass. We smile in return, especially at the young ladies who occupy the back seat! Still we are climbing and the road becomes more rough and the country more hilly. On our right is a deep valley with the Walden Beck rapidly coursing its way to the lowlands and the music of its song and the tinkle of moorland streams are in the air. We open a gate for a sturdy young dalesman on a spirited horse. He is clad in the familiar khaki which we see everywhere, no matter how secluded the place we visit. We stop to speak to him but the horse is fretful to go. So, "Cheerio, friend!" The road is now open to the boulder-strewn, bracken-clad fellside, where bleating moorland sheep scurry away on our approach. From the chimney of a farmhouse down in the hollow, there rises a curl of blue smoke. Here in 1914, we remember how we sheltered in a barn for over two hours when there was a terrific rainstorm. When there was no sign of an abatement, we returned to Aysgarth and caught the next train homewards. We would also put on record the kindly action of the farmer's wife who lent an overcoat to one of the party, telling him that he could leave it in the care of the station master. This, for an absolute stranger, mark you!

Beyond the farm, our road is nothing more than a grass-grown track running along the brow of the hill where there is a ridge of dark grit rocks. In attempting a short cut across a bend in the road, we almost make the blunder of which Mrs. J. had warned us. We realise our mistake in time, turn through a gate and follow the path to the summit of the hill. After ten minutes walking we decide to rest and fling ourselves down by a bed of bilberry. Here we sing the hymn of the Mountain Christians:

'For the strength of the hills we bless Thee,
Our God, our fathers' God;
Thou hast made Thy people mighty
By the touch of the mountain sod.
Thou has fixed our ark of refuge,
Where the spoiler's feet ne'er trod.
For the strength of the hills we bless Thee,
Our God, our father's God.

We are watchers of a beacon
Whose light can never die,
We are guardians of an altar
'Mid the silence of the sky.
The rocks yield founts of courage
Struck forth as by Thy rod.
For the strength of the hills we bless Thee,
Our God, our father's God.

For the dark, resounding mountain
There Thy still, small voice is heard.
For the strong pines in the forest,
Which by Thy breath is stirred;
For the storm on whose free pinions
Thy spirit walks abroad,
For the strength of the hills we bless Thee,
Our God, our father's God.

The eagle proudly darteth
On his quarry from the height,
And the stag that knows no master
Finds there his wild delight.
But we, for Thy communion,
Have sought the mountain sod,
For the strength of the hills we bless Thee,
Our God, our father's God.'

Today, our view is not as extensive as it might have been had the day been brighter and clearer. On our left we can still see Penhill, but from the rear, and the rest of the view is comprised of range upon range of heather-clad hills spread before us. Let those who will covet the 'freedom of the city' allow us the 'freedom of the moor' in all its many moods. Freedom and real life are here, even among the silent places. We do not attempt to explain the feeling of exhilaration which the moors impart to us, but it is there, a freedom from all the cares and worries of the world. We love the moors. At every season they have something in store for us. In spring, the heath plants putting out new leaves and we find the early crowberry, cowberry and red saxifrage. Summertime has found us lying on the heather, the heat-haze rising from the ground, whilst overhead the white cumulus clouds go sailing by in fleecy masses. We have hunted for the bog asphodel, the sundew and butterwort and listened to the musical drone of busy insects. But who can describe the glories of autumn? Who can depict on canvas that mass of purple bloom when the heather is in its prime? Can the artist give us the perfume of heather with his picture? Or make us feel the healthful breeze? Or depict a waving sea of cotton grass? Like the sea, there is something about a moor which cannot be described, but which must be felt; something primitive, wild and untamable as the creatures whose home it is. Especially is the rugged charm of this unfettered wildness felt in winter when, with a biting north-eater in our faces, we have battled with the elements and won our way at last to the site of an old beacon. Examples of the moor's ferocity we find along our way; a stone marks the place where, over a hundred years earlier, the moor claimed as victim one of the beacon guards — but that is another story. Today, we are in the midst of the Burton and Carlton Moors, desolate but grand! Everywhere we look, heather and tufts of wiry grass. Not a sign of habitation can be seen and man's handiwork is represented only by the few rough, gritstone walls and a shooting lodge on Deadman's Hill. Two or three hills intervene between us and this shooting box, which is our landmark for Nidderdale. The one place on the moor devoid of heather is the track we are following. This fades away in perspective as it ascends the opposite hill.

We have rested and eaten our chocolate, and now advance. Startled lapwings resent our presence and circle round uttering raucous cries. There is the shrill call of the curlew and with a buzz of wings the heavy grouse break cover and wing their way across the ling, cackling discordantly. We reach the head of a steep valley where the road diverges. We take the one to the right but afterwards learn that we should have followed the road down the valley. Passing through a gate, we cross the stream and visit some old coal workings where, a few years ago, a thin seam was worked but the only evidence we find of this industry is a few shaly mounds and a decaying wooden-wheeled bogie in an old hut. We climb the hill where our path, becoming more obscure, finally vanishes among the sphagnum moss. Continuing over the hill we strike Coverdale about a mile above Horse House. It has been worthwhile going out of our way to view the vale from this point. Coverdale is a narrow valley, fresh and green, running into the very heart of the moorland. Here, the little River Cover shows white against the green as it dances down the dale. Opposite to where we stand is our road, swinging pendulum-like up Arkleside Moor. Beyond, is Deadman's Hill and to our right, Little Whernside with rain clouds moving across its summit. In the valley on our left is a cluster of farm buildings and to these we now make our way. The weather is getting decidedly worse, the sky is leaden and we think we shall have rain. Climbing over a wall, we begin our descent into the valley as a timid rabbit scuttles away, turning a complete somersault in its haste. We slither down the steep meadow sides which are very wet and suddenly reach the Kettlewell to Middleham road which we follow down the dale to the cluster of buildings we had seen from the hilltop — the hamlet of Arkleside.

We wander round to the rear of a farmhouse and ask the farmer's wife if she can supply us with milk and food. She invites us to enter the parlour and provides us with milk, bread, biscuits and cheese. We drink all the milk she can spare, then she volunteers to make some tea. A little American organ is discovered in a corner of the room and soon the farmhouse echoes to the strains of music from six well-moistened throats. The farmer's wife is delighted with our song and assures us that if we had gone to Horse House we should have done well for there, they too are very fond of music. While we are singing, several children shyly peep through the little, square panes of the low window. If we appear to notice them they suddenly dodge out of sight, only to repeat their action later. It is here that the lance-corporal buys a small Coverdale cheese which he intends to carry home. We say it is a small cheese but before he has climbed Arkleside Moor, it weighs like the veritable Old Man of the Sea. To his credit, however, he stuck to that cheese like a snail to its shell, and eventually it was safely deposited on the larder shelf at home. In the kitchen range, a peat fire is burning and with the tongs the farmer's wife holds up a piece of the glowing fuel for our inspection. She likes a peat fire and, besides, coals are dear and hard to get. On this account she must economise in their use. She then shows us the peat house and looking down the dale, points out the village of Horse House and the church tower. This, as its name denotes, was once used as a posting establishment, a baiting place for horses when coaches rumbled through the dale to Kettlewell or, earlier still, when strings of packhorses climbed over the pass into Nidderdale. It is interesting to note that the valley gave name to the family of Coverdale. Here, in 1488, was born Miles Coverdale, Bishop of Exeter, whose

Deadman's Hill — Scottish traders and their packhorses.

translation of the Bible in 1533 was the first ever to be printed in the English language. Higher up the valley was born one James Metcalfe, carpenter, 1785. He eventually settled on the island of St. Helena and made the coffin in which the remains of Napoleon Bonaparte were conveyed to their last resting place in the vault of the Invalides in Paris. After thanking our hostess for her kindness, we leave the farm behind and climb the winding fell road to the bleak moor above. Now the rain commences and we don our capes. The road is good when compared to the one over the Burton Moor. It traverses a wilderness of heather and peat bogs lying between Deadman's Hill and Little Whernside. The scenery is rugged and there is a wild grandeur in the sight of the rain sweeping across the desolate wastes. On each side of the road, cut peat has been stacked to dry and everywhere are to be seen ancient peat cuttings dug out to a depth of between four to six feet. As the name suggests, a tale could be told about Deadman's Hill. In lawless times, bands of outlaws and robbers frequented these wild regions. The road was one of the routes travelled by Scottish traders with their trains of packhorses, but woe to the solitary traveller or ill-armed chapman, for they were robbed, beaten and often murdered by these ruffians. The victims were then buried in the peat bogs of this wild terrain, hence the name of the hill.

The descent into the valley begins and we are now in Nidderdale. In front of us is the Lodge Reservoir with the water pouring through its many sluices. The dam collects the headwaters of the Nidd and the wall which holds back the water is a fine piece of engineering. On the hillside opposite are temporary buildings and huts of the workmen and a little tank-engine is puffing up and down a railway track. Our road leads us into the valley and across the river. There is no bridge but we cross by stepping on large stones. Presently we reach a small barn where we shelter from the rain and there consume another ration of chocolate. When the rain abates somewhat, we proceed down the valley past a farmhouse and over the railway track to where there is a good road. We could follow this road to Lofthouse but decide to keep to our old trail over the moors, thus cutting out the bend in the valley. We climb the shaly track by the side of a disused gritstone quarry to the rain-soaked moor where the track is nearly obliterated by the moorland growth. Further on, we find the road again, this time well-defined, running between two walls. It is sandy and straight and we push on rapidly. The wind is blowing strongly and there is much rain. Our capes

Lofthouse station, 1920s.

drain off the greater part of the water but this drips onto our knees and our puttees are almost sodden. Hungry and thirsty as we are, the road seems endless but, welcome too. Below us, the valley of the Nidd and a great sheet of water — the Gouthwaite Compensation Reservoir. We pass through the bleakly situated village of Middlesmoor with its strongly built houses then down a narrow path by the old churchyard where a red-faced man is busily chipping away at a tombstone. After crossing a few fields, we come to Lofthouse, and there in front of us is a railway station! We saunter onto the platform, a bedraggled crew. A minister and his wife are sitting on some luggage, disconsolately watching the falling rain. They inform us that a train is due in ten minutes time and so we wait. Then the corporal discovers a notice which states there has been an alteration in the timetable and that the next train will not be due for an hour. We inform the reverend gentleman of this revelation — he looks as if he would like to swear — then the station master comes bustling along. The notice is correct and so we leave our baggage in his possession and resolve to get some tea. Not far from the station is a hotel where we obtain a first class meat tea. In the big dining room are two pianos, one is open and soon the colonel is busy on the keys, but the instrument is badly out of tune.

The other is in a corner behind a couch and it is found to be a really nice toned instrument. The obstructing couch is removed and a seat is provided for the colonel who, after a few preliminary flourishes, proceeds to play Beethoven's 'Moonlight Sonata'. We settle down for a treat but our joys are cut short by the entrance of a servant who tells us that the piano must not be played as it does not belong to the house. Now, had the colonel been playing 'rag-time' the request would have been understandable, but then this was real music! They were evidently not Dalesfolk!

Whilst we wait for the arrival of the 'express' on which we are to have the luxury of a ride, we will read an extract from W. Riley"s novel, 'Olive of Sylcote'. The scene is set somewhere lower down the dale but it is descriptive of the railway and the arrival of the train which puffed into Lofthouse station a few minutes after we had booked our tickets.

"At that moment the 4.15 panted into the little station, for the valley allowed itself the luxury of a railway, though it was only a light accommodation line that began where the East Yorkshire ended at Headley Bridge two miles lower down the line.

It was built for the convenience of the corporation that con-structed the huge reservoirs on the moors above, rather than for the benefit of the Dalesfolk, and a service of four trains each way on weekdays and none at·all on Sundays, was considered sufficient for the valleys requirements. The three or four carriages that com-posed the train were rather musty and antiquated, and it was not often that they were uncomfortably crowded, but the fuss the little tank-engine made as it puffed along was very impressive and calcu-lated to convey a false impression of the weight it was pulling."

Our engine is reversed and we take our seats in a musty, dusty, third-class compartment. On the dirty woodwork are written many unofficial notices, some witty, some 'muddy'. The following are samples of the funny ones:

'Passengers who get out to gather flowers while the train is going at full speed, do so at their own risk. They might get left!'

'While passing through the country, carriage doors should be kept closed to prevent cows from straying into the compartment.'

'This train travels at 60 miles an hour, more or less; mostly less!'

The station-master comes to the carriage window to say that we had better move into a first-class compartment, as further down the line, the 'thirds' will be filled with navvies returning from work and their clothes will not be overclean. Our social status thus suddenly advanced, we move into more salubrious surroundings. One of the occupants of this first-class compartment is the red-faced man whom we saw, earlier in the day, working in the churchyard at Middlemoor. He is a monumental mason from Pateley Bridge. The last passenger has arrived, there is a shrill blast from the engine and we are off. We get into conversation with the monumental mason and as the train rumbles leisurely along he points out various places of interest en route. Here is the overflow of the Gouthwaite reservoir with its line of spouting cascades. At the next station the train is invaded by the navvies, as predicated by the station-master at Lofthouse and two or three of them enter the sanctity of our first-class. Passing through Wath, we observe the tiny church and shortly afterwards we enter Pateley Bridge. It is about six o'clock and still raining! Our red-faced companion walks with us and promises to put us on to a good hotel where we can stay the night. Looking at the straggling, narrow street with its numerous, overhanging inn signs, we feel confident of obtaining lodgings. The first place we try is full, but next door we are successful. We are shown to our bedrooms and one contains a wardrobe exactly like the one we found in the Richmond 'House of Mystery'. We order dinner for eight o'clock, bathe and change into dry clothes and once more feel refreshed.

The weather has a stormy look about it and frequent showers prevent us from exploring the old town beyond a walk up the steep thoroughfare which is the main street. Opposite a disused brewery we get into conversation with two men who give us much information concerning the town and its surroundings. One has just told us how he crossed Deadman"s Hill with a bicycle during a snow-storm! The other is relating the dangers of Greenhow Hill which we can see directly in front of us. An old man of Shylockian countenance now joins us and listens to all that is said, nodding agreement the while.

This old chap tells us how he was once 'going' up Green'how 'ill' when he met a cyclist coming down at terrific speed.

"E weant get round that bend, I ses, an' 'e didn't! 'is front wheeal went smack agean a gert stun an' 'e flew up i' t'air as heigh as these 'ouses."

"What happened then?" we asked.

"Oh! 'is bike wer smashed to bits!"

"And the cyclist, was he killed?" we query.

Pateley Bridge High Street.

"Well nearly," says old Shylock, "but I rubbed 'im till 'is breath cam back agean!"

During this conversation, a man carrying a spade stops to listen. He looks as if he too would like to yarn, but as dinner will be ready we leave the group. The meal is excellent and we do full justice to it. Later, our friend, the monumental mason, passes the place and starts chatting to some of the party in the doorway. A well-built fellow now arrives on a bicycle; he is about 'three sheets to the wind'! Between his hiccoughs he tries to persuade the mason to stand drinks for the boys.

"You know," he says to one of us, "Hic! He's plenty of money, hic! He's a tombstone maker."

We tip the wink to our friend, telling not to take any notice of the beery one. He understands. The inebriated individual is nonplussed.

"Struth!" he exclaims. "You won't?" I'll tell you what I'll do, hic! You pay for drinks all round, hic! and I'll go another, hic! How many are there? One, two, four, six, eight, hic! How much is that? Eight pints is. . . .is. . . .seventy-six, hic! Seventy-six pence is. . . .five and tuppence. Will you do it? I'm not drunk!"

The maker of tombstones remembers he has other business to which he must attend and wishes us goodnight. The remainder of the evening is spent in the parlour singing our favourites and for some time we have the company of our would-be benefactor. He challenges us to a singing contest and introduced us to a companion, a well-dressed man of genial disposition who, according to the intoxicated one, is the finest baritone in the whole of Yorkshire! They are all members of a glee party and he indicates several more friends who have just come in. He then begins to talk about music, saying that in a certain piece which we had sung, we did not get that 'minor fifth'. In vain the colonel explains to him that there is no such thing as a 'minor fifth', but he knows differently. The baritone companion now asks us to sing a hymn and suggests, 'Lead, kindly light'.

"Hie! Don't sing that," says the beery one, "or they'll think we're all canned!" Nevertheless, we do sing it to his evident disgust.

His friends now persuade him to go home. He has a ten miles ride and has no lamps on his bicycle. Although he is drunk, his friends say that he can ride his machine better than he could walk. For us, another stroll up the street is enough, then we go to bed.

DAY EIGHT... SATURDAY

PATELEY BRIDGE TO GRASSINGTON

The last day of our holiday begins very dull and cloudy and the hills are wreathed in mists. We have had breakfast and paid our bill and now spend a few minutes buying postcards. Before leaving the district we should like to see those fantastic, weather-worn rocks at Brimham which are to be found about four miles south-east of Pateley Bridge, but our time is limited and so we must leave these for a future time. We cross the river and our rucksacked figures attract the attention of the idlers on the bridge. We now begin the ascent of Greenhow Hill and it takes us a full hour to reach the summit and the windswept village which takes its name from the hill. This morning, the only person we meet is a big-boned farmer with his horse and cart. Slowly they come down the road with the cart brakes screeching and the wheels skidding. Greenhow is the highest village in Yorkshire, standing at an altitude of 1,320 feet above sea-level. It is the scene of one of Rudyard Kipling's stories, 'On Greenhow Hill'. The houses are stolidly built of the native gritstone, as they need to be to withstand the blustering storms of these bleak uplands. The few green fields that have been wrestled from the surrounding moorland, remind one of an oasis in the desert. The moor is dominant again and stretches away for miles on either hand. Its surface is broken by gullies, the result of centuries of rainstorms. In places, black peat is stacked and from a distance the stacks resemble druidical remains. We have just had a heavy shower but there are signs of a better day; the wind is freshening and a patch of blue sky becomes visible. Now three or four charabancs pass us en route for Lofthouse. The freedom of the moor is upon us and we march blithely along this straight but undulating highway. By a gate is a little cabin with a notice which reads, 'Stump Cross Caverns'. We decide to visit them and an old man who has only one hand is ready to be our guide. First, he shows us his stock of postcards, then he lights a powerful acetylene lamp and gives us each a candle in a holder.

Hebden C.H.A. Hostel, the Six friends.

Leaving our coats in the hut, we follow the old man into a pit-like entrance and down a flight of steps cut into the rock. The light of day is left behind and the air becomes chilly. Our guide leads us along tortuous paths occasionally stopping to point out the finer examples of incrustation. Sometimes he uses his light to show the transparency of some curtain of stalactite. Now he strikes a fluted column with a piece of wood, causing it to emit several melodious notes. This he calls the 'Organ'. Then we come to the 'Chapel', a lofty chamber where we sing two hymns, then forward to the "Chamber of Pillars" where we have to stoop very low. This is our farthest point and we return; the old man swinging his lamp on his hooked arm and our candles casting weird, fantastic shadows as we follow the guide to the open air again.

These caverns were discovered in 1860 by William Bowes and David Gill during a search for lead. They are very interesting and well-worth a visit, particularly in view of more recent discoveries. But the incrustations are neither so fine nor so white as those in the Ingleborough Cave at Clapham.

Out on the road once more, we find that the sun is beginning to shine and the clouds are being scattered by the strong breeze. Reaching the top of the last, long rise, we get splendid views of Wharfedale with the old familiar contours and landmarks. Here we see Barden Fell and the reservoir, Rylstone Fell and the rounded knoll of Elbolton with the grey hills of Malhamdale in the distance. To the north there is Great Whernside. Looking back, we observe the long, straight road we have just traversed. It is interesting to note that this is the road over which John Wesley rode from Grassington to Pateley Bridge on the 1st May, 1780. The road now descends rapidly. We cross the little River Dibb by Dibbles Bridge. The moor is left behind us and farms, fields and meadows take their place in the picture. A young lady emerges from a gateway carrying a large can of milk. One of the party whose name we will not mention — except to say that he carried a Coverdale cheese in his rucksack — now gallantly offers to carry the aforementioned can for her. Gladly, she accepts his services and away they go in advance.

We enter the village of Hebden, but here we are unable to get anything to eat. So we at once made for the C.H.A. Guest House where we are given a hearty welcome by the manageress, and being old C.H.A. members, we feel immediately at home. We enjoy a good lunch and afterwards adjourn to the Common Room for a little music. Whilst talking to the genial manager, we find that the previous week he, too, had been in Swaledale and had occupied the very cottage at Muker where we had spent such a pleasant evening. On leaving the Guest House, our path now leads us down to the River Wharfe opposite the swing bridge*, but we walk upstream on the right bank of the river to Linton Church and forward to the Linton falls. Today, the river is full to the brim, rushing along irresistibly, a heaving current of swirling water. Linton falls are especially grand, the peaty water is literally churned into a mass of foam during its short, but tempestuous passage between these jagged rocks. The very bridge itself, vibrates with the shock of the charging current. Above the cataract, several fishermen have cast their lines in the calmer water of the river.

A few minutes walk brings us to the main road and the railway station of Grassington. We book our tickets, take our seats and the train moves off immediately. We are only just in time! Thus ended our holiday among some of the lovely dales of Yorkshire. A proper holiday, say we, and one that can be looked back upon with real pleasure.

---

*This, in reality, is a very narrow suspension bridge.

CONCLUSION

For freedom of action, the walking tour takes first place; no strandings or systematic studying of timetables In the words of the song, 'Well, you don't much care if you're on the right road, when you're bound for Nowhere Town'. Fresh air, fresh scenery, fresh faces are the order of the day. Every evening a fresh adventure when we seek a place of repose and how we do appreciate it when it is found!

But the most satisfactory feature of our holiday was the 'Trail of Song' which we took into the most likely and unlikely places. We have sung in church, cave and inn; we have dared to lift our voices even among the silent places of the hills.

Everywhere, our song was appreciated and we have yet to find the unmusical Dalesman, if there be such a person. The joy of life and our joy of living as expressed by song, was transferred to others. Not as 'ships that pass in the night' were we, for we fully intended that our presence should be felt. Should there be a 'next time', we know that we shall be assured of a welcome at any of the places we have mentioned, and the Dales are surely none the worse for our having passed through them.

How many people know the beauties of the country we have so vainly tried to describe? There is a false idea prevalent, that to have a good holiday one must spend half the time on a railway journey, and the further one goes from home, the better holiday one must necessarily have. Some day, such people will awaken to the fact that there is beautiful country even near home. They will find that they have been living on the edge of a wonderful garden, but of its proximity they are ignorant.

Now that we have stated our idea of a good holiday, "Wodz-yours?"

PART TWO

THE ODYSSEY — AS IT IS

1993

GRASSINGTON TO BUCKDEN

Distance: 11 miles (17.2 Km.)

Maps: O.S. Outdoor Leisure 10 Yorkshire Dales Southern Area

O.S. Outdoor Leisure 30 Yorks. Dales Northern & Central Areas

As the reader will gather from the original account, the Sturdy Tramps did not walk this section of their planned route because of 'very vile' weather conditions. Had they done so then they would probably have had to extend the holiday by another day in order to complete the first stage as far as Hawes, a distance from Grassington of almost 24 miles. There is a bus service between Skipton, Grassington and Buckden but this is not very frequent and subject to daily variations, usually determined by various market days. Check the current timetable before setting out!

For those who have the time it would be a pity not to walk the path, part of the long distance Dales Way, between Grassington and Buckden. As far as Kettlewell this is a comparatively high level route over well drained limestone terrain, whilst from Kettlewell onwards the path follows the course of the River Wharfe in the valley bottom. Because comment on this section of the route was omitted from Horace Pawson's account, I have taken the liberty of describing it in greater detail than perhaps will be apparent when dealing with subsequent stages of the walk.

The village of Grassington is often referred to as the 'Capital of Upper Wharfedale'. Certainly it is a very busy centre for tourists and has become a desirable place to live for many retired people and younger folks also who are prepared to commute often quite long distances by road to their places of work. The small bus terminus is directly opposite the National Park Information Centre where there is a large car park, picnic area and toilets. By the side of the cobbled square along Main Street is the small Folk Museum depicting various aspects in the life of the farming and lead mining communities in Upper Wharfedale in earlier days.

To commence the actual walk to Buckden, go to the top of Main Street to the Devonshire Institute and Town hall, turning left along Chapel Street with the Methodist Chapel on the right. Carry on to the very end of this

On leaving Grassington!

street, passing Town Head, (there's a 'Town Head' in virtually every Dales
village) and into a farm yard. A finger post directs the walker to the left
towards the cow sheds and the silage store. Negotiate this area and look
for another sign post with two arms, one indicating Grass Wood, the other
Conistone. Follow the way indicated by the latter, through the middle of
three gates then through three stone stiles in reasonably quick succession
to enter a large area of open pasture. Here two paths diverge, one veering
left towards the boundary wall of Grass Wood — a botanist's paradise in
Spring and early Summer. Ignore this path and keep to the broader track
which gradually closes with a wall on the right hand side. The area is one
of numerous limestone outcrops between which countless sheep tracks
and rabbit runs have been scoured. For the next two miles or so the path
continues in a northerly direction in an almost straight line with good stiles
along the way. Shortly before coming to Conistone Dib there is a fine
example of a field lime kiln to the left of the path. Now disused for many
years, the scorched stonework can still clearly be seen if one looks in at
the top of the kiln.

On approaching Conistone Dib the path ascends a short but gentle
slope between two limestone scars. At the head of the Dib is a narrow cleft
in the limestone through which a path makes an interesting descent to the
village of Conistone from where it is possible to take another field path

or lane back into Grassington. At this point, the Dales Way crosses the bridleway from Conistone to Middlesmoor in Nidderdale, a village to be visited towards the end of the Sturdy Tramps' trek. Immediately ahead, but slightly to the left of the path is an unusual landmark, Conistone Pie, a large, square shaped block of limestone surmounted by a cairn of stones. From this vantage point in clear weather conditions one can enjoy what

Coniston Dib, Wharfedale.

Grassington Folk Museum.

I consider to be one of the finest views in the whole of the Yorkshire Dales. Below in the valley bottom is Kilnsey with its massive overhanging crag, looking small from this height but shaped through glacial erosion thousands of years ago, whilst stretching away behind Kilnsey is Mastiles Lane leading towards Bordley and Malham. But looking in a north-westerly direction is the magnificence of Littondale with its steep fell sides, limestone escarpments, a cloud swept background and the River Skirfare meandering along the flat bottom of this valley to end its identity as it merges with the Wharfe just below but out of sight of where the viewer is standing.

The path ahead is clear, the stiles well maintained and eventually, on approaching an area of woodland, the Dales Way bears left, descending towards and joining the lane leading to Kettlewell. Set back on the right hand side is Scargill House, a very pleasant conference and holiday centre belonging to the Anglican Diocese of Bradford. A short distance further along the lane one has the choice of arriving in Kettlewell either by continuing along this same lane or by sticking to the Dales Way which re-enters a field on the right and passes through a series of long, narrow walled pastures so typical of Upper Wharfedale.

Kettlewell is much smaller than Grassington but boasts car parking facilities, toilets, hotels, guest houses, a Youth Hostel, and one or two shops. Many of the cottages are holiday lets and as in so many other villages throughout the country, young people have had to leave the area in order to find houses which they can afford. Nevertheless, it is an interesting village and a focal point for a number of shorter walks as well as being the starting point for a steep, narrow road which leads the walker or the motorist over into Coverdale, yet another dale later to be visited by the Sturdy Tramps.

Between Kettlewell and Buckden the meandering of the River Wharfe is so tortuous that had the footpath literally followed the course of that river then the length of the walk would have been considerably extended. Instead, the Dales Way approximates to the line of the Wharfe along its left bank as one looks up the dale. From the village, cross the river by the road bridge and immediately to the right is a gateway just beyond which is a finger post indicating the direction of Starbotton and Buckden. The path is well used and the hiker should have no difficulty picking out stiles and gateways leading from one field to the next. It is as well to note that from late Autumn to early Springtime this side of the dale with its steep north-east facing flank receives only the minimum of sunshine.

For any who wish to make a short diversion at the site of an old ford (GR.952745), a new footbridge spans the river allowing access to Starbotton where refreshments may be obtained at the local inn. A meeting point for pack-horse routes from Ribblesdale and Littondale to the west and from Coverdale and Wensleydale to the east, Starbotton was almost totally destroyed in the late 17th Century by a devastating flood surging down Cam Gill. During the next 150 years the village was gradually rebuilt, particularly when the lead mining industry reached its peak towards the end of the 18th Century.

The Dales Way continues close to the river, eventually crossing the Hubberholme road just outside Buckden. Like Kettlewell, Buckden offers all the basic amenities required by the present day hiker or visitor, including a number of purpose built self-catering cottages. There is also a National Park information point where one can obtain details of accommodation offered at any of the farmsteads between Buckden and Gayle. There are no other villages en route!

BUCKDEN TO HAWES

Distance: 12³/₄ miles (20.5 Km.)

Map: O.S. Outdoor Leisure 30 Yorks.

Dales Northern & Central Areas.

The narrow road from Buckden taken by the Sturdy Tramps was, in earlier centuries, a monastic route then a coaching road between Lancaster and the north-east. In 1920 it was still roughly surfaced and badly drained, its prime purpose being to link the various farming communities along the way. Today, although no wider than it was so long ago, except for passing places, it is a good surfaced road used by motorists and small lorries as well as by farm vehicles, but it is not suitable for coaches or towing caravans. However the Dales Way is adequately signed and well used and so the hiker is recommended to follow this path as far as Oughtershaw. Having refreshed one-self in Buckden return to the point where the Dales Way enters this lane and continue by entering the field on the right after crossing the little bridge. It is worth commenting on the work that has to be undertaken from time to time in order to contain the river in its course and to prevent bank erosion. Evidence of such can be observed along this stretch of the Wharfe between Buckden and Hubberholme. Horace Pawson described the Wharfe as a 'River of Moods' The author of this present commentary would heartily agree with that sentiment having, on occasion, seen the river rise by as much as eight feet in 12 hours, only to recede just as quickly. So, providing the Wharfe is not too high, the footpath through the fields should present no problem, emerging once again into the lane before arriving in Hubberholme.

Horace Pawson paints a very vivid word picture of the George Inn and the Parish Church of St. Michael & All Angels which needs little from me by way of updating. Although undoubtedly modernised internally, the 'George' still retains the warmth and atmosphere experienced by the Sturdy Tramps, with food, drink and accommodation still available. To enter the inn one has to go round to the back of the building and a word

Hubberholme, The 'George' Inn.

of warning to the 'townie' unfamiliar with the language of the Dales. The outside toilets are labelled 'Y'Ewes' and 'Tups' so make sure you know to which category you belong before entering! Until 1965, the George Inn was owned by the church, part of the building once being the vicarage. A centuries old custom is still enacted in the inn on the first Monday in the New year when a 16 acre pasture a little higher up the dale and which remains the property of the church is let to the highest bidder. The length of time taken for the bidding is determined by a candle which is lit at the commencement of the bidding and ends when it burns itself out.

Cross the fine arched bridge and go into the church which originated as a forest chapel in the late 11th or early 12th Centuries. Look for the things mentioned by Horace Pawson but also observe more recent additions of interest. The plaque to the author and playwright J.B. Priestly who died in 1984 and whose ashes rest in the churchyard. He described Hubberholme as 'one of the smallest and pleasantest places in the world'. The pews and other furnishings were made in 1934 by Thompson, 'the Mouseman' of Kilburn, his device being a mouse which is carved on many

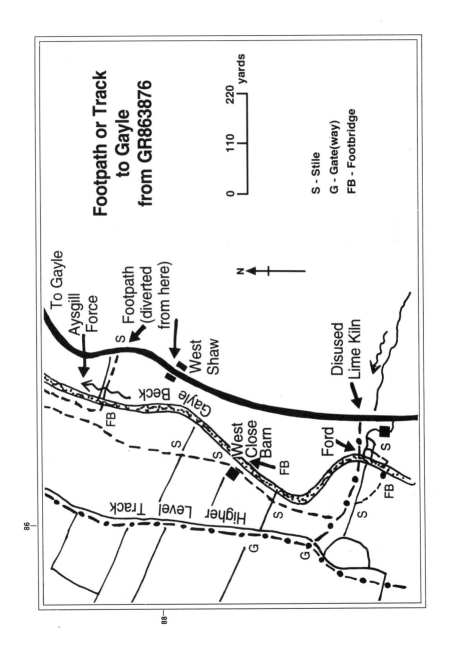

Footpath or Track
to Gayle
from GR863876

0   110   220

yards

S - Stile
G - Gate(way)
FB - Footbridge

N

To Gayle

Aysgill
Force

S   Footpath
(diverted
from here)

West
Shaw

Disused
Lime Kiln

Gayle Beck

FB

West
Close
Barn

Ford

S

S

FB

S

Higher Level Track

FB

S

G

S

G

86

88

Hubberholme Church.

of the pews. On the south wall close to the altar is the most modern of
the stained glass windows (1970) which, very briefly, depicts the history
of the church. To be seen in this window is Thomas Lindley, wrapped up
against the elements and riding a white horse. For many years during the
first half of the 19th Century he was minister and teacher at the little church
and school at Halton Gill in Littondale as well as incumbent at
Hubberholme. He would ride over Horse Head Moor from Halton Gill in all
weathers to take the service in St. Michael's Church. It is said that the
sexton of the Hubberholme church would stand on top of the tower
looking up the dale until he caught sight of Thomas Lindley before ringing
the church bell to summon the parishioners to worship. Close by this
window, but set into the floor, is the brass to which Horace Pawson refers
commemorating the short life of James Tennant.

The Dales Way now goes behind the church, climbing slightly then
dropping down to the river. A track which continues up the hillside leads
to Scar House. This 17th Century farmstead was once a meeting place for
local Quakers during the time of religious persecution. Many were imprisoned and died for their faith in York Jail, one of their number, James
Tennant (a common name hereabouts) being buried in a small enclosure

The 'Woodd' Spring, near Oughtershaw.

at the side of the house. At this point, due to the steepness of the fell above the Dales Way, the path is inclined to become rather wet after heavy rain owing to numerous small rivulets flowing into the Wharfe. Keep an eye open for the dipper, that dark brown but white breasted bird to be seen perched on rocks in the river, bobbing up and down, or diving into the water in search of food. At Yockenthwaite, originally a Norse settlement, where the six friend attempted to barter for a duck, note yet another beautifully proportioned arched bridge over the river. Deepdale, less than a mile ahead and where the Dales Way crosses to the opposite side of the river was, in monastic days, the site of the largest hunting lodge within what was then Langstrothdale Chase.

It is at Beckermonds, the meeting of the Green Fields and Oughtershaw Becks, that the River Wharfe truly begins. Here, after crossing a stout footbridge immediately upstream of the confluence of the two streams, the Dales Way rejoins the road. After ascending the steep rise, look for the little well described by Horace Pawson. It is on the right hand side of the road, water issuing from a fissure in the limestone and flowing into the carved stoned receptacle. The iron drinking cup has gone although the chain to which it was attached is still there. Perhaps what is more unfortunate is that the inscribed bronze plaque has also been removed leaving only the nails by which it was secured to the rock. However, above the well is the rowan tree under which the group sheltered, the original trunk shattered and stunted but with a fine secondary growth of branches.

Oughtershaw Hall on the left was built at the end of the 18th Century and it was the various members of the Woodd family who lived there who were responsible for the Victoriana one finds in this tiny community:- the aforementioned well; the Memorial Chapel, later to become the village school but no longer so; the memorial fountain for Queen Victoria's Diamond Jubilee and, on leaving Oughtershaw, the cross commemorating that monarch's Golden Jubilee in 1887! Limited overnight accommodation is available but there is no shop or post office — only a telephone kiosk! It is here that the hiker must make the decision whether to continue in the footsteps of the Sturdy Tramps and follow the ascending road ahead, or whether to extend the route by 3 1/2 to 4 miles over more difficult terrain by sticking to the Dales Way westwards to Cam Houses, there turning north to join the Pennine Way to Gayle and Hawes. This latter route is clearly shown on the map of the Yorkshire Dales Western Area, O.S. Outdoor Leisure Map 2.

The road route is pleasant (if the weather is likewise) with not much traffic except, perhaps, at weekends or during the peak of the Summer holiday season. For quite long stretches it is open to the moorland fells and one is able to walk along the grass verges. From the summit by Long Slack Gate there are magnificent views in all directions, particularly towards the southwest with flat topped Ingleborough standing out starkly against the skyline. The uphill slog is now over and a short distance further the road is joined from the left by Cam High Road, an old Roman Road to Bainbridge which shortly veers to the right in the form of a green track. At this point the road to Hawes suddenly descends a one in five gradient into Sleddale which is spread out below. Approximately 1¼ miles ahead there is the opportunity to take to the fields again for the last 1³/₄ miles to Gayle. By Busk limekiln (GR.863876), which is actually below the level of the road, a rough track to the left descends steeply to Duerley Beck where there is a ford. A short distance upstream is a good footbridge reached by going through a stile on the left just above the ford. After crossing this bridge, should the ford be too deep, go diagonally across the field to find a stile in the wall to the right. On going through the stile look for a gate and another stile straight ahead by the beck side, with a barn at the far side of the next field. Here there is a second footbridge, to be ignored, but yet another stile on the other side of the barn. Take this stile and follow the footpath which leads to a third footbridge to be seen in the distance at the approach to Aysgill Force.

After prolonged rain this route could be extremely wet and muddy underfoot. In such conditions, after crossing the first footbridge and the adjacent field, it would be preferable to rejoin and proceed to Gayle along the well defined track which crosses the ford and continues at a higher level. Alternatively, by going along the road some 150 yards beyond West Shaw farm, from where the path has been diverted in recent years, a ladder stile leads the hiker to the third footbridge mentioned above with a waymarked path to Gayle and from which splendid views of Aysgill Force may be obtained.

On arriving in Gayle it is well worth spending a little time looking at the old cottages which huddle around the ford, noting how the beck cascades over the broad but shallow limestone shelves on its way to join the River Ure, flowing through the centre of Hawes before this merger can be accomplished. For the hiker, Hawes is no more than a ten minutes walk from Gayle. No doubt the Sturdy Tramps, were they still alive, would be bemused by the sheer volume of traffic that throngs the main street today, the vehicles of visitors often outnumbering those of the residents, many of whom earn their livelihood by catering for the former. Not only is Hawes a centre for those wishing to tour the Dales, it is also a convenient stop for those in transit, being almost mid-way between the east and west coasts. Nevertheless, farming and the many associated service industries continue to play an important part in the economy of this small town. The long-time home of the famous Wensleydale cheese, the creamery in Hawes was recently abandoned by the large national dairy concern which owned it but, to the relief of locals to whom it offered employment, has been resurrected as a small independent firm to produce and market this delicious product. The Crown Hotel where the friends took their rest still offers refreshment and accommodation although 'piped' music has re-placed the piano on which the 'colonel' gave his recital over seventy years ago. Before leaving Hawes, whether by car or on foot, for those wishing to learn more of life as it was in their area, a visit to the Dales Countryside Museum is a must and is to be found adjoining the National Park Information Centre situated in the former railway station yard. This is a most suitable spot from which to commence the next stage of the route taken by the Sturdy Tramps.

HAWES TO MUKER

Distance: 8¹/₄ miles (13.2 Km.)
Map: O.S. Leisure 30

The route out of Hawes as far as Hardraw, no more than 1¹/₄ miles, is basically along the Pennine Way, partly on the road but mainly through the fields coming into Hardraw almost opposite the Green Dragon Inn. To view Hardraw Force, the 100 foot waterfall described by Horace Pawson, one still has to go through the inn but it will cost the visitor rather more than the fourpence charged in 1920. Nevertheless, the fall is well worth a visit particularly following heavy rainfall. Take waterproofs with you if you wish to go to the foot of the fall when in full spate!

It is no longer possible to climb above the fall by a series of steps as described and a return through the inn and onto the road must be made. By the side of the 'Green Dragon' more recent accommodation, the 'Green Dragon Apartments' has been added. At the right hand side of the entrance to this annex is a cottage with a signpost indicating a footpath to Simonstone Hall and which takes the walker actually through the tiny yard of the cottage. By following this path the Buttertubs road is reached in about ten minutes. As was the case with the route between Oughtershaw and Hawes, so it is with that between Hardraw and Thwaite in Swaledale. Other than taking the Pennine Way which adds some miles to the route and which is not really recommended for the purpose of this book, there is no alternative but to stay by the roadside. However, a short distance along the road from Simonstone Hall, some relief can be offered for any who wish to leave the highway for a short time. Just before coming to some recently built cottages on the left-hand side of the road, take the path indicated by the sign 'Shawgill Woods'. This is a short woodland walk along both sides of the beck with a footbridge at each end of the route. Immediately before the first — downstream — bridge, notice a small iron gate on the left with a 'No Access' sign. Probably this would have been the way the friends came after climbing above Hardraw. It is a matter of personal choice which side

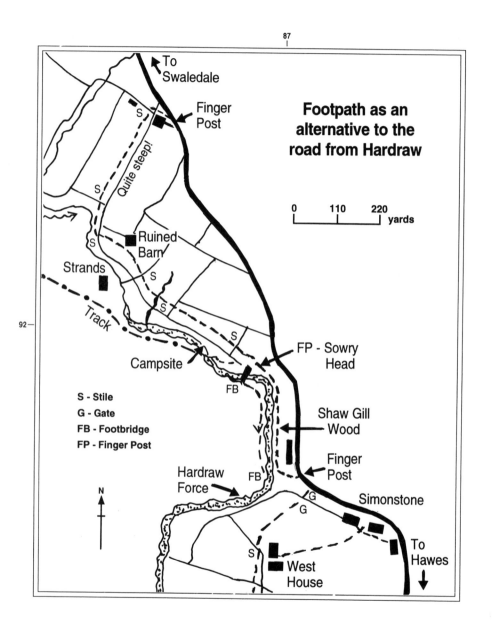

87

To Swaledale

Finger Post

Footpath as an alternative to the road from Hardraw

S

Quite steep!

S

0   110   220
|___|___| yards

Ruined Barn

Strands

S

S

92

Track

S

S

Campsite

FP - Sowry Head

FB

S - Stile
G - Gate
FB - Footbridge
FP - Finger Post

Shaw Gill Wood

Finger Post

Hardraw Force

FB

Simonstone

N

G

G

To Hawes

S

West House

Hardraw, looking south.

of the stream is followed but the upstream footbridge is rather fragile and may cause anyone of a nervous disposition some anxiety if the beck is in full flood! If this should apply to you, keep to the east side of the stream. However, this particular bridge is due shortly to be replaced by a new one, so perhaps by the time you get there, all will be well. Close to this upper bridge is a ladder stile leading onto the track which goes to two farmsteads, Strands and Fossdale. Turn right and about 100 yards ahead is Shaw Ghyll Farm with a finger post indicating the footpath to Sowry Head. The path is quite clear and adequately waymarked and after walking for some 500 yards a ladder stile adjacent to the stream takes one into a steep hillside pasture. Follow the path along the wallside to a gate and stile by one of two small barns at the upper end of this field, bearing right for a few more yards before access to the Buttertubs road is gained (GR867925).

One has to remember that in 1920 this was a grit road with most vehicles using it still being horse drawn. Today, more traffic will be encountered but nevertheless the road is open on either side until the descent into Swaledale begins and walking along the grass verge is not unpleasant. It is a long, steady ascent to the summit some 1725 feet above sea level and by the roadside tall marker posts are still in evidence to guide travellers through fog and winter blizzards. The hot weather experienced by the Sturdy Tramps as they progressed along this road was, perhaps, preferable to the wind and rain which all too often sweeps across these fells. The views as one reaches the summit reflect the harsh nature of the terrain; mile after mile of treeless peat and heather moorland with Great Shunner Fell to the west and Lovely Seat to the east. Close to the road are to be seen, here and there, spoil heaps, reminders of a once flourishing lead mining industry.

The bleak moorland gives way once more to softer limestone scenery when the steep descent to Buttertubs is reached and where, today, there is parking space for a few cars. The road now follows the flank of a limestone escarpment which drops away steeply to the right and from hereon the road user is protected by a strong fence or wall but with little or no grass verge for the walker. The field barns which Horace Pawson likened to block houses on the battlefields of France and Belgium are to be seen wherever one looks in the Upper Dales of North Yorkshire and form an integral part of the landscape. They date from the age when cattle had to be housed, fed and watered over the winter months in such buildings and when much of the farmer's day was spent in going from one barn to the next. With modern farming practice many of these buildings are surplus to requirements and where they have not been converted into places of residence many have fallen into a state of disrepair. Steps are being taken by the National Park Authority to encourage farmers to put

Thwaite! An oasis in sight!

some of these barns to alternative uses, basic bunk barn accommodation being one example.

I am sure that the Sturdy Tramps would be delighted with Thwaite could they see it today. No longer is it the desolate, neglected place they found on their arrival in 1920. Improvement has been brought about not by any upturn in the lead mining industry, for the mines never did reopen, but by a thriving tourist trade and the demand for self catering accommodation. In size, Thwaite is as it was seventy years ago but most of the cottages have been renovated and modernised inside and out but without spoiling the character of the settlement. The Temperance Hotel at which the friends obtained refreshments is no longer in business although the premises still exist. I was given to understand by one of the older residents that it was the building on the left hand side after crossing the bridge on entering the village. Set in the gable end is a letter box with the 'V.R.' monogram and close by are the stone mounting steps formerly used by horse riders. You can't miss it! But should you be hungry and thirsty after your trudge over the Buttertubs, don't despair! Almost opposite to what was the Temperance Hotel is a most acceptable 'watering hole' in the shape of the Kearton Guest House and Restaurant. Open for most of the year it is an establishment noted for comfort and excellent food, with the added bonus of a fine view of Kisdon Hill from the dining room.

'A pleasant lane tinged with the bright blue of the meadow geranium' is how Horace Pawson described what is now the metalled highway which all traffic must use when travelling along the length of Swaledale. The hedges are still tinted with the wild rose and meadow geranium (i.e. meadow cranesbill) but it is preferable for present day hikers to use one of the well-trodden footpaths or bridleways adjacent to this road as they make their way down the dale. The riverside footpath is quite distinct as one leaves Thwaite by the lane between Kearton's and the cottages opposite. After a few yards the Pennine Way diverges to the left and begins the climb around the eastern side of Kisdon, but for Muker the hiker proceeds straight ahead.

Although some of them will have been met earlier along the route from Grassington, now is an appropriate moment to write a few words about 'squeeze stiles', many more of which are soon to be encountered. These narrow stiles set in the dry stone walls and often constructed with curving upright stones making them even more narrow, must surely have given the

Squeeze stiles can be hazardous!

Lancashire artist L.S. Lowry his inspiration for the 'matchstick people' of his paintings! Designed and installed many generations ago to allow the farmer easy access to the numerous field barns as well as providing a short, direct route from 'A' to 'B' for the villagers, the stiles also had to restrict the movement of sheep and lambs from one field to the next. Hence the 'bowed' uprights frequently observed. So for the hiker who may be no more than five and a quarter feet in height, perhaps a little overweight from the waist down and carrying a large rucksack, be prepared for a tussle at each stile!

About halfway between Thwaite and Muker the path joins the road at Usha Gap Bridge only to re-enter the fields a few yards further on by Usha Gap House and Camp Site. One has only to look at the numerous footpaths, bridleways and byways converging on Muker to realise that at one time this small village was the focal point for social and business life in Upper Swaledale. It had a church, a Methodist Chapel (rebuilt since the Sturdy Tramps worshiped there), a Literary Institute and a school. The school no longer functions as such but plaques on the outer wall commemorate its two most outstanding scholars, the brothers Richard and Cherry Kearton. Richard (1862-1928) was a naturalist, author and lecturer, whilst Cherry (1871-1940) in addition to his older brother's attributes was also an explorer and pioneer of wild life photography. One of the byways with rather macabre associations is the 'Corpse Road', a mediaeval route of some 14 miles from Keld to Grinton Church which had the only consecrated burial ground in Upper Swaledale until Muker Parish Church was built in 1580.

Muker, in common with other villages throughout the dale, caters quite adequately for the needs of visitors whether they are staying in the area or simply passing through. It is not evident from Horace Pawson's account just who 'Mrs. H.' was, but the two cottages in which the Sturdy Tramps were accommodated are probably amongst the group clustered around the post office which is set back from the road up the incline by the Literary Institute. It is from this post office that the next stage of the journey commences.

MUKER TO REETH

Distance: 11 miles (17.6 Km.)

Map: O.S. Outdoor Leisure 30

Two signposts to the right of Muker's little post-office indicate the way to go; first, a simple footpath pointer, followed by a yellow way-marked sign 'Gunnerside and Keld'. The Ordnance Survey map indicates a path which crosses the River Swale by a ford but the hiker is advised to follow the one going in a northerly direction through some half a dozen small fields until Ramps Holme footbridge is reached. The fields are typical hay meadows which were a common sight throughout the length and breadth of the upper dales until recent years but which have now almost disappeared through the application of selective herbicides and the move towards silage production rather than hay making. In June and early July, these small meadows present a carpet of colour with buttercups, clover, wood cranesbill, stitchwort, yellow rattle, speedwell and many other wild flowers. On experiencing such a scene at first hand, one can well appreciate the sights and scents described by Horace Pawson as the group made its way down the dale. As with field barns and dry stone walls, farmers are being encouraged to maintain some of these hay meadows in selected areas of the Dales, they being accepted as a major factor in the character of the landscape.

On crossing the footbridge over the River Swale the path bearing left makes its way to Keld but to the right one immediately has the choice of a high level or low level route to Gunnerside. Both are clear and easy to follow, the former being a good byway on the north side of Ramps Holme Farm and Calvert Houses and from which can be enjoyed splendid views across Swaledale, whilst the latter is the riverside footpath with numerous 'squeeze' stiles to negotiate. This lower path leads the hiker to Ivelet Bridge, an ancient, beautifully proportioned, high arched pack-horse bridge over the River Swale and which is associated with the Corpse Road mentioned earlier. It has been suggested that the large, rectangular stone slab which is to be found set in the ground on the north side of the bridge was where coffins were placed whilst the bearers had a rest! From this point the hiker follows the lane to the hamlet of Ivelet before entering the fields again and continuing to Gunnerside. For those who, initially, take the high level byway, it is possible to descend to the low level route either at Calvert Houses or by Gunnerside Lodge.

The Sturdy Tramps did not visit Gunnerside itself where, today, there is a small car park, toilet facilities and places of refreshment. Like Thwaite and Muker, Gunnerside also had strong connections with lead mining and along the upper reaches of Gunnerside Gill there is much evidence of this industry in the form of old mine shafts, crushing and smelting mills and the attendant spoil heaps. Lead ore mined at various levels underground was often carried, via other levels, long distances before being brought to the surface to be treated. The remains of the Old Gang Smelt Mill (GR.955014) between Gunnerside Gill and Hard Level Gill, are now maintained in a reasonable state of preservation by the National Park Authority. Visitors to the area wishing to learn more about the lead mining industry by undertaking local walks are recommended to look at specific 'Walk Cards' prepared by the National Park and also the 'Footpath Map and Guide to Upper Swaledale' by Arthur Gemmell, (Stile Publications, Otley). These cards and guides are also available for other parts of the Yorkshire Dales.

It is not without significance that in Earby, the home town of the Sturdy Tramps, there is to be found a small but extremely comprehensive Mines Museum housed in the Old Grammar School. The Earby Mines Research Group has been in existence for many years doing, as its name suggests, research into and some restoration of many of the lead mines that are to be found in the Yorkshire Dales. In the course of this work, numerous artefacts have been collected and models constructed, all of which are displayed in the museum.

By leaving Gunnerside along the road as though going back up the dale, it is possible once again to follow the actual route taken by the Sturdy Tramps for the next 2½ miles. On crossing the river, the road bears right up a short but sharp incline where it is met by the narrow road from Crackpot. In the angle of this junction is a track through a gateway with a bridleway sign to Grinton. This is the 'sequestered grass grown lane' described by Horace Pawson, possibly less of a lane now than it was seventy three years ago but nevertheless a route that can still easily be followed. The pleasant fragrance of aniseed from the decaying leaves of the sweet cicely was also much in evidence when I walked this route some time ago, as were vivid splashes of purple from banks of the lesser knapweed. A word of warning however! Should the river be in full spate there is the possibility of the lane flooding in those places where it is, quite literally, within a few feet of the low-lying river bank. Eventually, the bridleway becomes a much better defined route known as Dubbing Garth Lane before joining the minor road from Crackpot and Summer Lodge, then crossing the river at Isles Bridge. As one ambles along this track from Gunnerside it is not difficult to visualize the scene where the friends caught the horse to be mounted by the 'colonel', or the site where they had their picnic and were entertained by the 'adjutant' with his disastrous egg throwing demonstration.

On crossing the Swale at Isles Bridge, is obvious that the Sturdy Tramps continued along what is now the main road to Reeth. Horace Pawson relates how, after passing through the hamlet of Low Row, they stopped

The Punch Bowl Inn, Feetham (the ficticious 'Bluebell').

at a spot where 'above us, on rising ground, it is the Blue Bell Inn'. Enquiries have revealed that although at some earlier date there was an inn at Low Row, there is no record of there ever having been a 'Blue Bell Inn' in that area. But the siting of the inn 'on rising ground' fits perfectly that of the Punchbowl Inn at Feetham only a few hundred yards beyond Low Row. This hostelry has been in existence for over 300 years, evidenced by the date stone 'R.W. 1638' whilst high up on the front wall is also to be found an excellent example of an early fire insurance plaque in the shape of Britannia. Because he was so accurate in naming other hostelries visited during the holiday, one can only assume that when it came to writing his account Horace Pawson had forgotten the actual name of this inn, hence the fictitious 'Blue Bell'.

The road along the dale is rather busy and not very wide, so it is suggested that hikers who may have refreshed themselves at the Punchbowl should retrace their steps to Isles Bridge where a footpath to Reeth is indicated. For quite some distance this path goes along the raised bank of the river until it ascends to the road at Feetham Wood. Less than a quarter of a mile along the road, on the left hand side, the path enters the fields again as far as Healaugh where once more it switches to the opposite side of the road on leaving this village. Here there are two paths, one going down to the riverside, the other diverging slightly from the course of the road. The latter is the more direct route although both paths merge a short distance before entering Reeth along an old lane.

In July, 1920, the Sturdy Tramps experienced difficulty in finding accommodation for the night in Reeth, the largest of Swaledale's villages, and we are told that 'year by year it is gaining in popularity as a place for holiday'. That popularity has been continuing and increasing now for over seventy years, so if it is your intention to stay there during the peak of the holiday season, do reserve your accommodation well in advance. Reeth is an excellent centre from which to explore the surrounding district; Arkengarthdale to the north, leading over into Teesdale; Grinton to the south with its ancient church and roads to Wensleydale; eastwards towards the gentler hills around Richmond, whilst the nature of the countryside to the west has already been described. It should be noted that there are limited bus services along and around most of the Dales, particularly during the summer season, and by judicious planning it is possible to contrive a full day's walk in a particular direction, then catch a bus for the return journey at the end of the day. The six friends did eventually find shelter at Arkle Mill House which was by the side of Arkle Beck. This was the house adjoining the old mill and today is known simply as 'Mill House'. It would appear that a number of dwellings have been, at some stage, created from this building which, of course, no longer serves its original purpose. These dwellings are distinguished by rather unusual lintels in the shape of half millstones which given the appearance of large, protruding eyebrows above the windows they protect!

It has become the fashion in recent years in many rural areas, to remind residents and visitors alike of how life used to be lived, since so much is changing so rapidly, often being replaced by a rather drab level of uniformity, resulting in the loss of regional character. Swaledale is no exception and the small Folk Museum in Reeth, with an adjacent Information Centre, open from Easter to the end of October, is to be found set back from the spacious village green on its left hand side as one leaves the village for Richmond. Looking eastwards from the green down the valley, indicates the direction one must take to accomplish a further stage in this odyssey of the Sturdy Tramps.

REETH TO RICHMOND

Distance: 10½ miles (16.8 Km.)

Maps: O.S. Outdoor Leisure 30 and
O.S. Pathfinder 609 (NZ 10/SE 19)

The bulk of the traffic today between Reeth and Richmond follows the B6270, the 'modern' road constructed in the 1830's. Prior to that decade, the only suitable route for vehicles was the upland coach road via Marske. This was the way chosen by the Sturdy Tramps but in 1920 it was still a sandy, grit surfaced road. Today it has a metalled surface and is used mainly by local traffic, although during the summer holiday season it is liable to heavier usage. Nevertheless, it is a satisfactory road along which to walk, more like a country lane, with rather steep gradients out of Low Fremington and into Marske but, as Horace Pawson remarked, "This is a fine, breezy walk over the uplands . . .". It is suggested that today's hiker might prefer to join the lane about half a mile beyond where it diverges from B6270 at Low Fremington. This is achieved by taking the signed footpath to High Fremington which is on the left after crossing Reeth Bridge, then continuing beyond the hamlet until the coach road is reached (GR.055988). An interesting alternative to the first section of the route is to continue along the main road to Low Fremington, bear left onto the coach road, eventually taking the narrow byway to Marrick Priory. From there, a green track bears left by Steps Wood and continues to the village of Marrick where Crook Bank Lane eventually joins the coach road again at a crossroads (GR.074994).

Marrick Priory, now a residential youth centre for the Diocese of Ripon, was originally a house for the black-robed nuns of the Benedictine Order, the whole of the surrounding pastureland and Marrick Village itself belonging to the priory. The track from the priory to the village as it passes through the wood is an ancient stone paved, stepped path known as the 'Nuns' Steps', hence Steps Wood. On the opposite side of the River Swale a little way down-stream where stands a more recent farmstead is the site of

93

Ellerton Priory, another nunnery but one which belonged to the white-robed sisters of the Cistercian Order. Both establishments were closed down during the Dissolution of the Monasteries in the early years of the 16th Century, although Marrick survived some five years longer than its neighbouring priory.

As the six friends sang their way along this upland route they observed 'a chimney like object among a clump of trees'. This is to be seen on a hill top to the right shortly before descending into the village of Marske and the tall obelisk, for that is what it is, Hutton's Monument, marks the grave of Matthew Hutton who died in 1814. Marske and the land around it belonged to the Hutton family for a number of centuries and later generations lived at Marske Hall (now flats) which was built around 1750. Half way between Reeth and Richmond, the village is surrounded and sheltered by beautiful woodland which flanks the sides of the glen through which flows Marske Beck. The feeling one gets on arriving at this spot is encapsulated in the description given by the late Jessica Lofthouse in her book 'Countrygoer in the Dales':- 'Marske is unlike any other village in these dales. There is an air of some cosy caught-in-a-combe Cotswold community around the Big House.'

As in Thwaite, the Sturdy Tramps took refreshment at the Temperance Hotel which no longer exists. I suspect that it was the large house on the left hand side of the road with the sun dial on the wall and in front of which is a seat awarded to Marske in 1971 for the Best Kept Village. The only public facility in the village today is a tiny post office, so walkers are advised to carry their own refreshments. Marske is, nevertheless, a splendid place to rest particularly should the more exposed parts of the route be rather more than mere breezy!

If you, the hiker, are happy with the lane along which you may have walked to Marske then by all means continue along that same route taken by the 18th Century stage coaches on their way to Richmond. It is an undulating road, again rising to breezy heights after crossing Clapgate Bridge, giving one a much greater panoramic view of the countryside than would be possible from the 'new' road by the Swale. Just as the long descent into Richmond beings, keep an eye open on the left hand side for the beacon mentioned by Horace Pawson, 'the basket-like arrangement of iron hoops on a pedestal', clearly to be seen at the spot aptly named Beacon Hill. It is many, many years since the Georgian race-course at Low

To Richmond — the old coach road.

Moor was last used for that purpose. The starter's box and remains of the grandstand are still in evidence, whilst close by are much newer stables for the training of horses.

However, there is a very acceptable and most varied alternative to the old coach road which takes the walker along what is part of the Coast to Coast Walk described by the late Alfred Wainwright in his book of that title. Less than half a mile after leaving Marske by the old road, look for a finger post on the right hand side of the lane indicating 'Richmond, 4½ miles'. The waymarked footpath goes diagonally across two or three fields before descending steeply to a footbridge over Clapgate Beck, then climbing up the hillside towards a white painted cairn where a well-defined hard core track is joined. It would appear that the ascending footpath from the footbridge is used more by sheep than by human beings! Whilst crossing the fields before coming to the bridge, look back at the lower hillside on the opposite side of the road recently left to see a splendid example of 'lynchets', the terraces created by Anglian farmers during the 8th and 9th Centuries. These were strips constructed to make for easier ploughing on a hillside, the plough often being pulled up to four pairs of oxen. Lynchets are to be found in many parts of the dales, a reminder of times long ago when communities had to be self-sufficient, growing arable crops on land which would be considered totally unsuitable for that purpose by most farmers today.

The bridleway now to be followed goes through an area known as Applegarth and runs roughly parallel to the road taken by the Sturdy Tramps. But between the two routes are impressive and, in places, well wooded limestone scars. From Applegarth Scar the hillside drops steeply to form one side of the deep valley through which meanders the River Swale and the 'new' road, mentioned earlier, with its vehicles looking like matchbox toys. A short distance beyond the point where the footpath merges with the bridleway there is an impressive stand of venerable yew trees, many of which are gnarled and disfigured through weathering centuries of storm and tempest. The track one follows is well used as access to farmsteads which also bear the name of Applegarth, 'West Applegarth' being the first such dwelling. Soon, Applegarth Scar gives way to Whitcliffe Scar and ahead lies Whitcliffe Wood. Before entering the wood, look up to the scar on the left to observe a monument to Robert Willance who, in 1606, came over the scar on his horse. The horse, it is said, was killed but Willance miraculously survived; the spot is now known as Willance's Leap.

On emerging from Whitcliffe Wood, the next farm is High Leases to be followed by Whitcliffe Farm where the track now has a metalled surface for the last mile into Richmond. Whether the hiker follows the route just described or takes the old coach road, one's first view of Richmond is dominated by the massive Norman keep of the castle. Just over one hundred feet in height, the keep is one of the three largest in the country, a most impressive sight not easily forgotten. The reader of Horace Pawson's account will have noted how he had an eye for the small items of interest encountered during the course of the holiday, as well as for the more dominant features. One such item, not seen by the six friends simply because it was not there in 1920, is to be found on the wall of a cottage close to where the lane from Whitcliffe Farm joins the Reeth/Leyburn Road (A6108) by West Field Post Office. It is a circular yellow and black plaque placed there by the Automobile Association in 1927 to mark the total eclipse of the sun in that year. The inscription reads, 'Solar Eclipse, June 1927, Centre Line of Totality'. Ranging between the insignificance of this reminder of an occurrence some 66 years ago and the commanding presence of the 900 years old Norman castle, Richmond has much to interest the visitor who is blessed with a sense of curiosity.

The other dominant feature of Richmond is its enormous market place,

(N.B. Saturday is market day), in the centre of which is the much altered 12th Century church of the Holy Trinity and an 18th Century obelisk which replaced an earlier market cross. Many of the early markets were established within the shadow of Norman castles. Richmond was granted a market charter in the same century as the building of the Holy Trinity, the tolls thus raised providing a useful source of income for the Earls of Richmond. The market place also serves as a bus terminus and the spot where excursion coaches drop their passengers. Consequently and because of the wealth of shops and inns around the square and the streets radiating from it, many visitors whose stay may be limited to no more than a couple of hours fail to see what Richmond has to offer beyond this central area. Therefore, for the curious who have only a short time to stay, make for the information bureau by the corner of Victoria and Queens Road, almost opposite the little Georgian Theatre, pick up for a few pence the town Trail Guide and discover some of the more obscure points of interest. You will not be disappointed!

"Beware of sheep!"

RICHMOND TO LEYBURN

Distance: 9¹/₂ miles (15.2 Km.)

Map: O.S. Pathfinder 609 (NZ 10/SE 19)

It is to be hoped that should you stay overnight in Richmond then you would find a more hospitable place than the 'House of Mystery' experienced by the six friends. What a pity that we don't know exactly where this dwelling was within the town, or indeed, that of the more convivial Mrs. P. . . who invited them to her home for the evening.

The description given by Horace Pawson of the walk from Richmond to Leyburn, and there is little alternative but to follow the route taken by the Sturdy Tramps, requires a little imagination on the part of the reader or by any latter day Sturdy Tramp. Not that he was misleading in what he wrote but simply that he could not have foreseen the changes that would occur in the years ahead. Leaving the town by Bridge Street and Richmond Bridge, an area of great character, continue a short distance along this rather busy road bearing right at the first junction signed to Downholme. Most of the traffic out of Richmond will continue ahead to Catterick. At the second junction it is the hiker who proceeds straight ahead in the direction of Brokes. This was the sandy, moorland route followed by the friends, at the end of which they met the two young ladies who enquired their way to Richmond. It is still a pleasant, not too busy lane to walk along, ascending gradually until the open moor is reached. Suddenly, the lane becomes a wide, first class road! Do not be surprised should you meet heavy battle tanks or if your ears are assailed by the sound of gunfire, for this is now one of the many training grounds over a wide area for those of Her Majesty's Forces residing at Catterick just over the hill to the east. For many years this centre has steadily expanded to become the largest garrison town in the north of England and provision for training has grown accordingly. This is made abundantly clear by the various Ministry of Defence red warning signs to be observed, given a touch of incongruity by agricultural notices urging one to 'Beware of Sheep'. Whether or not it

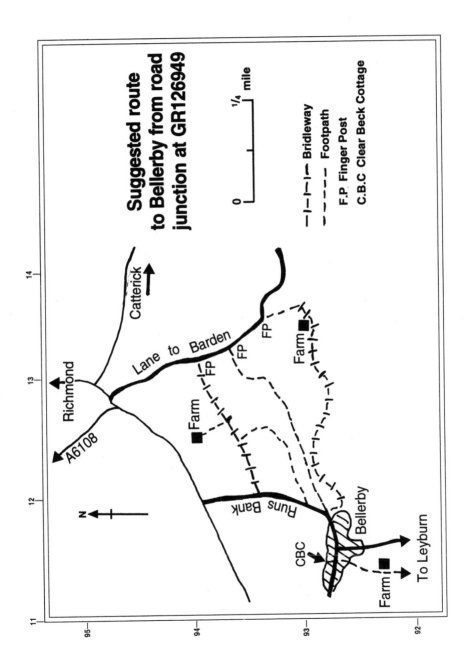

is deemed that the sheep will pose a threat to the marauding tanks, I am not sure! But no harm should befall the hiker who does not stray from this road or the wide grass verges alongside it, whilst the views to the north and the west across the River Swale compensate for the intrusion of the military from which the Sturdy Tramps were escaping so shortly after the first world conflict.

The descent off the moor is quite steep, bringing the traveller to a junction with the Catterick road from the left and, some 250 yards ahead, that with the main Richmond to Leyburn highway (A6108). However, rather than trudge along this busy road which is probably what the Sturdy Tramps did in less hectic times, it is suggested that today's hiker turn left down the lane signposted to Barden, just before the junction with the A6109. On the way along this lane, first a bridleway then a footpath are indicated to the right, the former close to a barn. These two tracks simply lead to the main road at the top of a steep hill called Runs Bank. Should you not mind the short road walk down this hill into Bellerby, then by all means take the bridleway. But less than half a mile further along the lane turns sharply to the left with a second bridleway sign indicating a track straight ahead. By following this route via Friar Ings, one comes directly into the village, a much more pleasant way than the main road it must be said.

Road signs warning drivers of oncoming traffic of the possibility of encountering cattle, horses, deer, children or even old people are quite common throughout the country, but how many times has the reader come across a notice, albeit unofficial, warning drivers to beware of ducks on the road? Such is the sight meeting those coming down Runs Bank on bearing right into Bellerby, for alongside the road as one enters the village is a narrow but very clear stream, home for numerous ducks which have a habit of squatting on, or waddling across, the main road! I am sure that the residents of Bellerby take their ducks very seriously and it is to be hoped that so too will passing drivers. The 'Cross Keys' visited by the Sturdy Tramps, still exists and continues to offer food and drink to the traveller but whether or not the little boys of Bellerby still cadge 'fags' for running errands is another matter.

There is no necessity for the hiker to complete the remaining distance to Leyburn by walking along the road since there is an adequate and distinct footpath which runs roughly parallel to the road. To find access to this path is not very easy for the first time visitor. From the village take

The Ducks of Bellerby.

the minor road passing the village store and a disused Wesleyan Chapel on the left, followed by a number of modern houses. On the other side of this road are some older dwellings in front of which flows the stream mentioned earlier. Opposite 'Clear Beck Cottage', between two of the modern residences, is a very narrow ginnel, easily overlooked, but at the far end of which is a stile leading into a small field where the footpath can clearly be seen. This continues by the west side of Manor House Farm, through a series of fields, entering Leyburn at the end of a residential cul-de-sac. Immediately across the avenue between the top two dwellings is another ginnel, then yet another leading down steeply to the main road one left at Bellerby alongwith its accompanying volume of traffic.

Leyburn is to the eastern end of Wensleydale what Hawes is to its western end, the focal point for business and social activities. A glance at the map will reveal that many roads converge on Leyburn from all directions making it a very busy place on most days of the week. At no time is this more evident than on market day, Friday, (Tuesday in Hawes), when the huge square is cleared of cars and becomes a scene of activity, packed with stalls selling all manner of goods, patronized not only by residents who come in from the surrounding countryside but also by the many visitors to the area. That Leyburn is a place to refresh oneself is clear from the number of hostelries to be found around the market square including, on the north side, the 'Golden Lion' where the Sturdy Tramps found accommodation.

It is obvious from the account of the visit to Leyburn that Horace Pawson was much impressed by what he had heard and read of the local antiquary William Horne, and the pleasure they all experienced in having the opportunity to view the historical artefacts that this gentleman had collected. Alas! On making enquiries of a local historian, I was informed that although Mr. Horne is still remembered, it would appear that all trace of his private collection has been lost.

LEYBURN TO WEST BURTON

Distance: 11¹/₄ miles (18 Km.) or 11³/₄ miles (18.8 Km.)

Map: O.S. Outdoor Leisure 30

Horace Pawson writes that on leaving Leyburn the group 'followed the main road by the Shawl Woods to Preston-under-Scar and then to Wensley'. This statement is somewhat puzzling since the main road (A684) out of Leyburn in this direction leads first to Wensley from where a minor road goes to Preston-under-Scar and Redmire. So it is unclear whether or not the friends did actually visit the former village. There is a pedestrian footwalk along the main road to Wensley but there are also two acceptable field routes as far as Castle Bolton with a difference in distance of no more than half a mile. The slightly longer way is via Wensley and Redmire, whilst the shorter takes a more direct line through Preston-under-Scar.

Take the footwalk on the left hand side of the A684 as it leaves Leyburn, passing the dental surgeries, as far as the junction with Low Wood Lane where a footpath into a field is indicated. This is the way forward shortly crossing the now disused railway line, with the path leading into a series of fields. It is apparent that in recent years some field patterns have changed with the removal of walls or hedges, the land being given over to arable crops. The path, however, even along the edges of the ploughed fields is reasonably clear until one comes to an old gate with a waymark sign, leading into a long, narrow pasture with a small barn to the right hand side. It is here that the path becomes obscure but by turning left immediately on entering this field and skirting the edge of it, another footpath will be met with a stile at each side of the pasture. By taking that over to the right (the left side stile goes back to Leyburn!), the route to Wensley is quite clear. It passes by a small field and copse which is a nature reserve known as the Old Glebe Field, then around the edge of the adjacent field and so into Wensley itself, often described as the most picturesque of the villages in Wensleydale. I feel sure that residents of certain other villages would dispute this claim! In the centre of Wensley it is impossible to miss

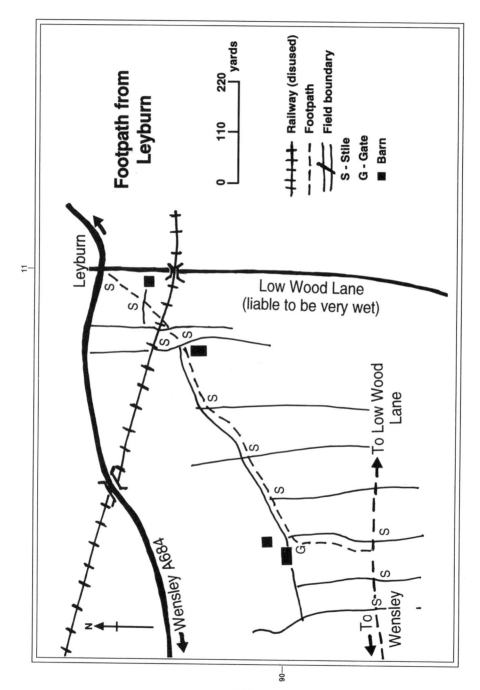

Footpath from Leyburn

the imposing entrance to the parkland of Bolton Hall, although the avenue of trees seen by the Sturdy Tramps has disappeared alongwith other wooded areas.

The concrete driveway as far as the Hall itself, although easy to walk on does present a rather disfiguring scar in otherwise idyllic surroundings. Bolton Hall, the home of Lord Bolton, was built in 1678 by ancestors who preferred something more comfortable than the huge draughty towers and rooms of Bolton Castle. Shortly after passing the Hall, the concrete drive gives way to a good but much rougher track which enters the woods ahead, climbing slightly to give splendid views of the River Ure below. At the end of the wood the Sturdy Tramps would have continued along this track as it turned to the right, eventually meeting with Wood End Lane. However, after emerging from the wood, there is also a footpath which goes straight ahead, through an old fashioned iron barred 'kissing gate', crossing a number of fields before meeting Well Lane, then Wood End Lane just as it enters the lower end of Redmire.

Horace Pawson twice makes a passing reference to the railway which once ran the length of Wensleydale linking with the Settle-Carlisle line at Garsdale Head in the west. For many years this line terminated at Redmire and was used only for mineral traffic from quarries north of the village to the main east coast rail route at Northallerton. Alas, even this section has now been closed, perhaps forever. In Redmire itself, accommodation and refreshments are available and there is a caravan site nearby. To complete the short but uphill walk to Castle Bolton, take the footpath which begins parallel to the railway track just north of the village. Access to this is obtained by following the minor road which passes the 'Bolton Arms' and a new residential development. There is a footpath sign close to this development but, as building continues, this could disappear in the not too distant future.

With the exception of the field path between Leyburn and Wensley, this was virtually the route taken by the six friends. But should you prefer a high level stroll with views which vie with any others to be seen on this tour, then the alternative along Leyburn Shawl should be your choice. 'The Shawl' as it is known locally, is the eastern end of a five miles long limestone escarpment which stretches from Leyburn to just north of Redmire. Preston-under-Scar, as its name suggests, lies at the foot of the steepest part of this escarpment and like many other villages visited on

Castle Bolton

this journey through the Yorkshire Dales it too developed during the lead mining boom of the 18th Century.

Access to 'The Shawl' is by a street off Commercial Square at the top (western) end of Leyburn Market Place, keeping to the left of a wall on the other side of which is a children's play area. It is a walk so frequently used by local people that it is impossible to get lost! For most of the first 1½ miles there is a wall on the right hand side over which can be seen a vast area of mainly disused quarry, whilst on the opposite side of the track, the tree covered escarpment drops away very steeply. At the right time of the year a wide variety of flora can be found along the side of the path. Keep to this track along the top of the escarpment until the very end of the woodland area (Warren Wood) is reached and one emerges into open pasture at a waymarked stile. Immediately the path, now less distinct, descends diagonally down the hillside first crossing a derelict field boundary with a squeeze stile still intact. At the second stile beyond this, the path merges with a farm track, passing the site of an old settlement before passing through a field gate set in a wall. Do not go through this gate since the footpath follows parallel with the north side of the wall until the track along the eastern edge of Gillfield Wood is reached. Should the weather be very wet then it will be advisable to follow this track to the narrow road which leads to Preston-under-Scar. However, under dry conditions the ·hiker might care to take a chance on what appears to be, on the O.S. map, a very direct footpath through the southern end of Gillfield Wood. But beware! On entering the wood directly opposite the field from which one has just emerged, the path begins to split into a multiplicity of tracks which cross numerous streams and rivulets which drain into this corner of the wood. It becomes a veritable maze, but should you be fortunate enough to find the correct path, this will lead to a stile in the boundary wall of the wood then across fields to the lane and the village. Rest here for a while to admire the views, but be sure to carry your own refreshments for these are not to be obtained locally. In Preston-under-Scar, ignore the road where it forks to the left down the hill but carry on to the very end of the village where there has been a slight footpath diversion in front of a large house. The diversion is clearly indicated, the path going through easy woodland again before joining the Richmond to Redmire road. Proceed down the hill to the junction with the road from Wensley and immediately on the right join a narrow lane which shortly gives way to open pastures on either side

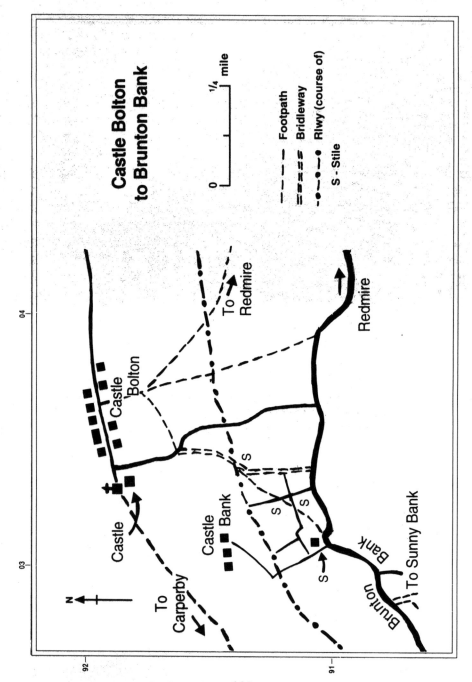

Castle Bolton
to Brunton Bank

0   ¼ mile

— ·· — Footpath
=== == Bridleway
— ● — ● — Rlwy (course of)
● S - Stile

To Carperby

Castle

Castle Bolton

To Redmire

Redmire

Castle Bank

Brunton Bank

To Sunny Bank

of this surfaced track. Ahead is the magnificent panorama of Upper Wensleydale with Penhill and the entrance to Bishopdale to the left. The end of the track is gated where it enters Hargill Lane, but directly opposite is the way to Castle Bolton and another fifteen minutes walk brings one into this hillside village which boasts a place of worship at each end. On entering the village, the ground floor of one of the very first cottages houses the Methodist Chapel, surely one of the smallest in the country. At the other end is the Anglican Church of St. Oswald, dwarfed and overshadowed by the massive ramparts of the castle but which it pre-dates by three-quarters of a century. Still used for worship, St.Oswald's is also a centre for exhibitions depicting aspects of interest in Yorkshire or in connection with ecclesiastical events. Some refreshments can be obtained in the tiny post office by the church, or in the castle if one is actually viewing the structure. Horace Pawson has written sufficient about the fortress for this volume but I am sure that he would feel a sense of satisfaction that much work is still being undertaken on the fabric to ensure that visitors can continue to enjoy and absorb the atmosphere he so vividly portrayed. (N.B. The village is Castle Bolton but the fortress is known as Bolton Castle!)

There are various footpaths from Castle Bolton to Aysgarth and from there to West Burton, but I have tried to keep as close as possible to those which I believe were followed by the friends. A short distance down the road from the castle a bridleway forks to the right, this shortly crossing what is the old course of the railway. Cross this and immediately on the right, tucked behind a tree is a stile. The path from this stile, although obviously little used, goes diagonally across three fields to meet the Redmire to Carperby road on a sharp corner close to some farm buildings. I found that under these circumstances a pair of binoculars is very useful for spotting elusive stiles! Now go along the road up a short but steep incline to the first farm track on the left which goes to a dwelling called Sunny Bank. About 100 yards along this track look for a stile, again difficult to see, in the wall over to the right, go through it and make for High Thoresby Farm. It was at this farm, I believe, that the friends witnessed the horse driven threshing machine in the spacious yard. A similar type of implement has been recreated in one of the rooms at Bolton Castle. On passing through the farmyard at the right hand side of a barn, the path has been diverted slightly. Instead of going diagonally across the small field as shown until recently on the O.S. map, cross it at right angles to the left hand end of the far wall where there is a signpost 'Castle Bolton-Aysgarth'. One field ahead in the Aysgarth direction is a second post indicating 'Carperby' but the footpath to Aysgarth via Hollin House bears diagonally left at this post. No difficulty should be encountered in following this path to the Falls.

In his account, Horace Pawson is not very specific about the route taken to Aysgarth, but it is reasonable to assume that after passing High Thoresby the group took the bridleway towards Carperby under the old railway bridge to Low lane, for he writes, 'On our right we observe the village of Carperby but our route is not in that direction'. Note that this bridleway appears to have been recently reinstated between Thoresby Lane to the east and Low Lane to the west for it is not shown on the earlier editions of the O.S. Outdoor Leisure Map 30. So for those wishing to follow this route rather than the path via Hollin House, continue straight ahead at the Carperby sign and join Low Lane where the track from Hollin House comes from the left. Some distance along the lane at the left hand side there is a stile with a finger post indicating Aysgarth. By following this clear footpath one avoids the narrow road to the Falls which, particularly in Summer, is very busy. But Carperby itself is well worth a visit for it vies with Wensley in its beauty.

Whichever route is taken one comes to Freeholders Wood which was purchased by the National Park in 1982 when a long term policy of woodland management was immediately implemented. Good paths have been installed alongside viewing points for the Lower and Middle Falls. An admirable leaflet giving full details of these Falls and the Woodland Trail is obtainable at the National Park Information Centre nearby and where there are car parking, toilet and refreshment facilities.

The Upper Falls can be viewed from the bridge which crosses the River Ure at this point. It should be noted, however, that the footpath from the bridge in an upstream direction veers away from the river alongside which there is no right of way and although the landowner will permit visitors to keep close to the river bank, a charge is now being levied on those who wish to do so. On crossing the bridge is the old mill to which reference is made, no longer grinding corn but serving as a Coach and Carriage Museum with a cafe alongside to cater for the many visitors who come to this spot each year. The steps by the mill lead up to the parish Church of St. Andrew where the Sturdy Tramps were unable to gain access because

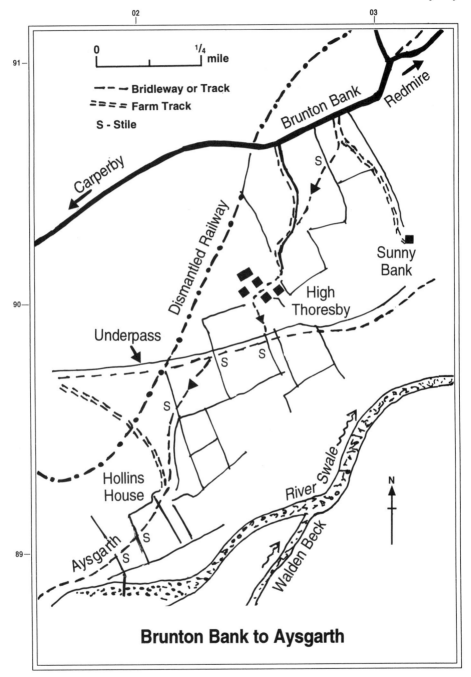

Brunton Bank to Aysgarth

In Aysgarth Churchyard

of earlier vandalism, obviously no new phenomenon. Although not as old as many of the churches in the Dales, St. Andrew's has one outstanding treasure — a magnificent, large painted screen which was the work of the Ripon Guild of Carvers in 1506. Originally placed in Jervaulx Abbey, it was removed from there thirty years later following the Dissolution of the Monasteries.

On leaving the church by the drive leading to the road from the Falls, look for an oval brass plate set into a rock at the foot of a tree on the right hand side of the drive. The inscription tells us that this plate marks the grave of John Wray of High Gill, better known as 'Deaf Jack', who died in July 1847 at the age of 82, followed by a short verse eulogizing his life. Cross the road to gain access to a footpath which passes through a series of small fields and into Aysgarth Village. I wonder how many visitors to the area call at the village post office today, as did the Sturdy Tramps, to collect their 'Poste Restante' letters and postcards? From the village there is no necessity to walk very far along the road. By the junction of the A684 and the minor road to Thoralby, almost opposite the garage and filling station, is a footpath sign indicating Eshington Bridge. The path beyond is well used and waymarked, shortly crossing a lane and quickly bringing the hiker to the head of a brow which presents one with the 'alluring prospect' described by Horace Pawson. A rapid descent to Thieves' Gill, a crossroad of footpaths, a short climb over a second brow followed by yet another descent to Eshington Bridge. From there a twenty minutes stroll along the footpath signed to West Burton ensures that another stage of the odyssey has been accomplished.

What was written about West Burton over seventy years ago is perfectly relevant today. Externally, little appears to have changed beyond minimal residential development at the top end of the village. There must be very few villages where the children can use the green in front of their school as a playground. 'The 'Black Bull' where the friends were refused refreshments no longer exists, the premises now being a private residence, but the 'Fox and Hounds' continues to cater for the visitor with food and accommodation of a very high standard. The old market cross and stocks are still in evidence although the mill from which the Wensleydale Dairy Company operated has now been converted into flats. A small car park occupies the area in front of the mill and almost without leaving one's car it is possible to view Mill Falls so aptly described by Horace Pawson. For readers not familiar with the Dales, ' a small scale Strid' in his description is a reference to a spot of that name near Bolton Abbey in Wharfedale, where the River Wharfe is suddenly funnelled into a very narrow, deep and dangerous cutting through the limestone. On a hot summer's day, the area around Mill Falls still provides the visitor with a haven of shade and tranquility, as indeed does the whole village which is set back away from the busy main road.

WEST BURTON
TO LOFTHOUSE

Distance: 13½ miles (21.75 Km.)
Map: O.S. Outdoor Leisure 30

This leg of the journey is basically along old packhorse routes. It will probably prove to be the most arduous of the whole circuit but also one of the most rewarding should the weather be favourable. The condition of the tracks varies from excellent to atrocious, the latter state particularly prevalent on the steep inclines in and out of the valleys due to water erosion. Take the Walden road which is signed at the top end of the village green in West Burton, climbing steeply as far as the junction where 'Walden North' and 'Walden South' are indicated. Follow the latter. Alternatively, just before reaching this junction there is a footpath to the left with the signpost 'Rockwith Bridge ¼ m; Cote Bridge ½ m'. At Cote Bridge there is a small site for caravans. For the next 1¼ miles the lane steadily climbs the side of the fell arriving at a steep 'S' bend where the name 'Whiterow' is set into a rock with a footpath sign to Bridge End next to it. It is probably Whiterow Farm to which Horace Pawson is referring when relating the incident of the loaned overcoat in 1914. At the top of the bend just beyond the cattle grid, the way forward is clearly indicated by another sign pointing to the left and proclaiming 'Bridle Road to Horsehouse and Kettlewell'.

No real difficulty should be experienced in following this bridleway to Horsehouse in Coverdale, although there are a number of points to watch out for, particularly should visibility deteriorate. A few yards beyond the gateway after passing an old railway van, now used for storage purposes, on the right-hand side of the path the obvious track veers also to the right. Ignore it! Look for the 'F.P.' and arrow painted in yellow on a stone straight ahead and follow the grassy track to the next gate where the bridleway becomes much clearer. Shortly after passing through this gate there is a

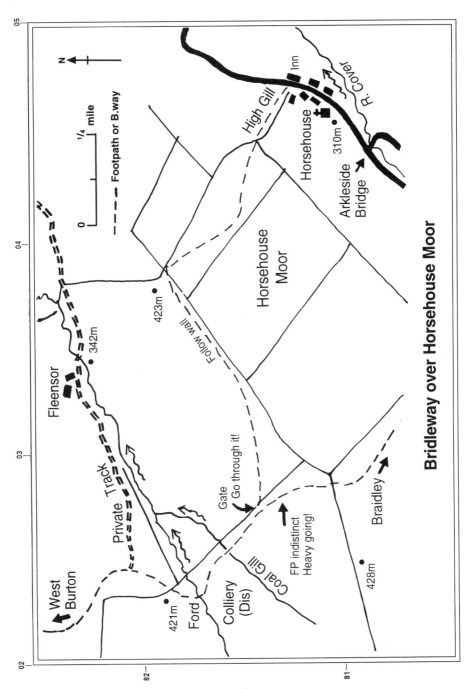

Bridleway over Horsehouse Moor

divergence of tracks. It would appear that it was at this point the Sturdy Tramps lost their way, for comment is made about taking the track to the right instead of to the left and descending into the valley. Today, at this junction, there is a very clear sign indicating that the track to the left is a private road to Fleensop. So what was an acceptable path for the hiker in 1920 is no longer permissible today and one must bear to the right to the ford which crosses a deep gill. Nearby are the old coal workings of Fleensop Moor, all that remains being a few spoil heaps and two well maintained stone huts obviously used by shooting parties during the grouse season. One can only marvel at the hardiness of those who had to earn their living by extracting a very poor quality coal from such desolate surroundings.

About a quarter of a mile after crossing the ford the track again diverges. The obvious route goes straight ahead, eventually descending into Braidley and then up to the dale along the road to Kettlewell. This is the path taken by the six friends, again I believe in error, for after a very short distance it becomes anything but clear, crossing peaty, tussocky clumps of vegetation interspersed with drainage channels making walking difficult even in dry conditions. The divergence of the tracks is not apparent until one realises that the way to Horsehouse is through a metal gate in the wall which is to the left of the path as it ascends from the ford. There is no signpost to indicate the way although an earlier traveller, probably as perplexed as I was, has tried to scratch direction marks on the wooden gate posts. Once through the gate the track is reasonably clear and straight but it does give one the opportunity to practise some compass work! It will be noted from the O.S. map that at a wall junction (GR.034815) a footpath is indicated making a hypoteneuse to the right-angle formed here by the bridleway. There appears to be no sign of this path or clear access to it and the hiker is advised to follow the bridleway along the wall side then through a gate and follow the steep descent by High Gill into Horsehouse.

There are a number of settlements along the narrow road which runs the length of Coverdale after it has climbed out of Kettlewell via Park Rash and descended Hunters Stone Bank. It could be said that Horsehouse with its church, inn, post-office-cum-general-store and a dozen or so houses is one of the larger communities but certainly it can offer refreshments and limited overnight accommodation. Indeed, this whole valley of the River

Cover has much to offer the visitor who is looking for a peace and solitude no longer to be found in the more popular and larger dales.

It is only a short walk along the road up the dale from Horsehouse to Arkleside. A lane branches to the left with a sign 'Unsuitable for motors' and just beyond this, a disused field lime kiln is to be seen by the side of the lane which then crosses the River Cover by Arkleside Bridge and into the tiny community of four or five dwellings. There is a small, uninhabited house on the left hand side, now used as a storage place, with a fine carved door lintel bearing the initials 'T.H.' and 'I.H.', presumably those of the first couple to live there, and the date '1687' although the last digit is not too clear owing to weather erosion. I wonder in which of these houses it was that the farmer's wife supplied the Sturdy Tramps with refreshments and from whom the 'lance-corporal' purchased a Coverdale Cheese?

The route from Arkleside which winds its way up the fell side and over to the Angram and Scar House Reservoirs is shown on the O.S. map only as a double dotted line and not the green of a bridleway or footpath as was that from Walden to Coverdale. Nevertheless, this is the correct track to take and as Horace Pawson remarked seventy years earlier, it is a much better defined route than the one over Burton Moor. However, it is steep and initially rather rough. To the summit of the fell is a distance of about 1³/₄ miles with an ascent of some 725 feet, so depending (a) on the weather or ground conditions and (b) one's own state of physical fitness, a minimum of sixty to seventy minutes should be allowed for this ascent. Stop frequently to admire the views — which is my excuse for regaining one's breath! About halfway up the hill a track shown on the O.S. map as a footpath leading to Deadman's Hill branches to the left. A notice informs the hiker that this is a private road! Peat is no longer cut as it was in the earlier years of this century but it is still possible to discern the outlines of the old diggings. In inclement weather this moor is indeed a most inhospitable place, for there is not a single scrap of shelter anywhere in sight. The fence and gateway across the summit, with the sharp rise of Little Whernside to the west and the aforementioned Deadman's Hill to the east, form part of the boundary of the Yorkshire Dales National park, Nidderdale being excluded from this area.

At the time when the Sturdy Tramps passed this way only Angram Reservoir had been completed, Horace Pawson referring to it as Lodge Reservoir, presumably after the settlement of that name (one farmstead

Scar Village, 1920s.

and a tiny Wesleyan Chapel) at the foot of the fell and which is now completely abandoned with little to show for it. The path to be taken after descending from the moors bears left towards a clump of trees which marks the site of Lodge and continues towards the huge masonry barrier at the end of Scar House Reservoir. The building of this catchment was commenced in 1921, therefore some imagination on the part of the reader is necessary in order to visualise the crossing taken by the group in 1920 but which is now under the waters of the reservoir. There would be a ford across the River Nidd below Angram Reservoir, alongside which would be the stepping stones to which reference is made. Whenever the level of Scar House Reservoir is sufficiently low, one can see quite clearly the walls flanking a track emerging from the water on the south side, forming a diagonal line to the bridleway to Middlesmoor and re-appearing on the north side slightly to the east of, but below, Lodge.

It is towards this bridleway that the hiker must now make by crossing the causeway which tops the huge wall of the dam. To the left, close to the public car park can be seen the foundations of the many buildings which formed Scar Village. During the years the reservoir was being built, (1921 — 1936) as many as 1100 people, workmen, wives and children lived in this village which catered for all their needs. At the end of the causeway turn right as indicated by the Nidderdale Way sign and after some 200 yards, left up a rough track, again with the Nidderdale Way finger post. This is the route taken by the Sturdy tramps and after a stiff climb the track levels out and begins a steady descent towards Middlesmoor. No matter what the weather conditions it is still a joy on the descent to see Gouthwaite Reservoir ahead. Some miles ahead to be sure but after the long, lonely crossing of the moors from Coverdale there is that feeling of relief at seeing more substantial signs of habitation once again. Middlesmoor, perched on a steep brow at the head of the valley, must have been a haven of refuge for the packhorse drivers of old.

The footpath from Middlesmoor to Lofthouse is by the side of the church yard wall and is very well defined, going by Halfway House (aptly named) and emerging into the road from Lofthouse. At this point another footpath to Nidd Heads bears left, crossing the narrow Water Authority road which leads to the reservoirs, then over an arched stone bridge spanning the infant River Nidd and into Lofthouse itself. The village, apart from more recent dwellings was built not along the Middlesmoor road but around the narrow moorland route to Masham in Lower Wensleydale. Quite near to each other in this old section of the village are two small structures which might just possibly have been seen by the six friends. Both relate to the First World War, one being a Victory Memorial Well and the other a War Memorial Fountain erected in 1920. The former has three dates carved in the stone:-

'War commenced, 4th August, 1914; Armistice signed, 11th November, 1918; Peace declared, 28th June, 1919.'

But in our present day health conscious society, surely the inscriptions on the Memorial Fountain deserve a prize!

'A pint of cold water three times a day is the surest way to keep doctor away. Who so thirsteth let him come hither and drink.'

and

'If you want to be healthy, wealthy and stout, use plenty of cold water inside and out! Let animal and man drink freely.'

My wife tried to follow these instructions but alas, the fountain was dry!

LOFTHOUSE TO PATELEY BRIDGE

Distance: 5³/₄ miles (9 Km.)
**Maps: O.S. 1:25000 Pathfinder 630 or SE 07/17
and Pathfinder 652 or SE 06/16**

Whether it was weariness after crossing three areas of moorland on leaving West Burton, or the very wet weather they encountered that persuaded the Sturdy Tramps to look for public transport from Lofthouse to Pateley Bridge, we shall never know. I suspect that it was a combination of the two factors since the walk down the valley is not too long, is most pleasant and not at all strenuous. The Crown Hotel where they enjoyed ' a first class meat tea' continues to flourish but whether or not the hotel still possesses someone else's piano, I couldn't say. The railway of course closed many years ago; on the 31st December 1929 to be exact as far as the public passenger service was concerned, with the whole of the railway stock being put up for auction in June, 1937 following the completion and opening of Scar House Reservoir the previous year. For railway buffs and any who wish to learn more about this line and the construction of the reservoirs, a small book, 'The Nidd Valley Light Railway' by D.J. Croft (Oakwood Press) makes excellent reading, whilst a range of photographs is usually on display in the Nidderdale Folk Museum at Pateley Bridge. There is no mistaking the building by the roadside in Lofthouse which was the station still with the platform intact at the rear. There are two more almost identical buildings in Ramsgill and Wath which were also served by the line.

The obvious route to follow to Pateley Bridge is the Nidderdale Way, although in some sections the direction of the path is obscure. A case in point is in Lofthouse itself where one had difficulty in gaining access to the path in the Pateley Bridge direction. It is much easier to follow the road out of the village for just over a quarter of a mile to the point where the Nidderdale Way, clearly signed, crosses the road. Take the path to the right

120

which shortly meets and follows the raised bed of the old railway track before recrossing the road once more. Here the path ascends to a gateway at the corner of the wood which can clearly be seen on the hillside and from which splendid views are obtained of Gouthwaite Reservoir and again up the valley to Middlesmoor perched on its hill. The path here is enclosed on one side by a boundary fence for the wood and by a stone wall on the other side, the only obstacles for anyone over five feet in height being long, overhanging branches putting one in danger of being decapitated! Make sure you go behind two farmsteads along the line of the path which eventually descends by an old sunken lane to Bouthwaite, a small community which has strong associations with monastic ownership in the Middle Ages. This connection is reflected in the names of some of the buildings — Grange Farm and Fountains Cottage.

The Nidderdale Way follows both sides of Gouthwaite Reservoir, the west side being along the road, the east side along or almost parallel to the course of the old line. This does tend to be a little confusing until it is realised that the northern extremity of this route is the loop it makes on crossing the causeway at Scar House Reservoir. The hiker who has come over from Coverdale will probably have noted the Nidderdale Way sign at the northern end of the causeway as well as at the opposite end. Therefore at Gouthwaite Reservoir the outward and return sections of this long distance path are simply on opposite sides of the valley. It is the path on the east side of Gouthwaite that is recommended, going by Covill Grange and Coville House Farms. Some three-quarters of the way along the reservoir side the bridleway diverges from the old railway track and climbs toward woodland on the left. With the barrier and causeway to the dam in sight, the bridleway is met by a track coming down the hillside from Lamb Close. On the right hand side a few yards ahead are two gates set at an angle to each other with a gateway some fifty yards further on. There is nothing to indicate the route but take the track through this third gate (GR.141686) leading down to the end of the causeway — no crossing permitted — where the footpath to Wath is waymarked. This path by the bank of the River Nidd is quite clear, joining and crossing the lane to Wath by the bridge over the river. From this point onwards the footpath is very well used, through fields and later quite literally going along the raised bed of the old line once again, coming into Pateley Bridge close to where the main road (B6265) crosses the river.

Horace Pawson doesn't say exactly where they stayed for the night in Pateley Bridge except that it was along 'the straggling, narrow street with its numerous overhanging inn signs.' There are still a number of places offering accommodation along the High Street and elsewhere in this small town. The walker coming along the route just described would also have passed a large caravan site just outside the town. In recent years, Pateley Bridge has begun to attract many visitors and for its efforts has won a number of national awards for floral displays. During the summer months particularly, the hanging baskets and old stone troughs are a blaze of colour and a joy to behold. Mention was made earlier of the Nidderdale Museum which is to be found in the former Rural District Council Offices (originally the workhouse) opposite the Parish Church and which, in July 1990, received the National Heritage Museum of the year Award for 'The Museum which does most with the least.' Official guide sheets relating to Pateley Bridge and the surrounding area, and which provide the visitor with ample information on places to visit, are readily available at the museum, the Information Centre on the main street and in various local shops.

A glance at the location of Pateley Bridge on the Ordnance Survey map in relation to the tightly packed contour lines running in a northwest to southeast direction on either side of the valley is enough to tell anyone that steep gradients are inevitable on approaching the town from either east or west. It is to Greenhow Hill on the west side of the River Nidd that the hiker must now address himself or herself in order to complete the walk undertaken by our Sturdy Tramps.

PATELEY BRIDGE
TO GRASSINGTON

Distance: 12½ miles (20Km.)

Maps: O.S. Pathfinder SE 06/16 (Grassington & Pateley Bridge)
or Pathfinder 630 and Outdoor Leisure 10

The worst section of Greenhow Hill is encountered immediately on leaving Pateley Bridge and is approximately two miles in length. The road which is not very wide, twists and turns, in parts attaining a gradient of about one in five. There is no footway alongside the road, neither are there any grass verges suitable for walking upon. The pedestrian, therefore, is advised to avoid it! This can be done quite easily without adding more than half a mile to the road route and along a bridleway which is certainly far less hazardous that Greenhow Hill itself. Turn right at the Royal Oak Hotel and at the end of a row of cottages, opposite a block of dwellings called Chapel Mews, turn left up a short street. The end of this street leads into a field through which runs a reasonably well-used footpath and which, in turn, after passing through a number of small gates and stiles joins the hard-surfaced bridleway already referred to. This links together a number of dwellings such as Riggs House, Hillend and Coldstones Farm and by following this very clear and much more pleasant route one eventually rejoins the main road opposite the entrance to a quarry (GR.122643) which is no longer disused as indicated on the O.S. map. At this point the hill has more or less levelled out into a gentle undulating stretch, with wide grass verges on either side of the road. Although this road can be quite busy and because of a dearth of alternative paths in the east to west direction, one has little option but to walk along it for the next 3½ miles if a visit to Stump Cross Caverns is to be made.

The areas of Greenhow Hill is one of numerous scattered dwellings which were built from the 17th Century onwards to house the lead miners and their families. Each house had with it a small holding on which the family could grow crops, keep poultry and raise a few head of livestock

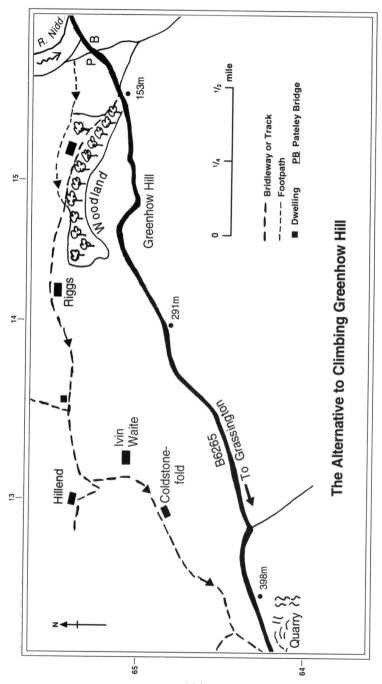

The Alternative to Climbing Greenhow Hill

in order to supplement the somewhat uncertain and meagre income received from mining. A study of the Ordnance Survey map will reveal that this whole area is dotted with disused mines and shafts. The mining industry came to an end towards the close of the 19th Century, the cottages becoming deserted and falling into a state of neglect. However, it is clear to see that many of these dwellings have now been rebuilt or renovated, taking on a new lease of life as holiday homes or even permanent places of residence for those prepared to commute to surrounding urban areas. Refreshments are obtainable at the Miners' Arms in Greenhow Village. Two things that have not changed in the seventy years since the Sturdy Tramps came this way are the splendid views afforded of the encircling fells and moorland and the sharp, invigorating atmosphere to be experienced (in spite of the internal combustion engine) as one walks along the road. But, be prepared for anything as weather conditions are liable to change very rapidly!

After reading Horace Pawson's account of the group's visit to Stump Cross Caverns, it is something of a shock to approach and visit them today. A large car park by the side of the road with an adjacent stone building housing all the paraphernalia deemed essential to attract today's visitor:- cafe, souvenirs, postcards, ice-cream, etc! Visitor access has been extended since 1920 and conditions within the caverns made much more comfortable. To quote the description given in the official guide for Pateley Bridge and Nidderdale:- 'Here the visitor may descend into a veritable fairyland of glittering stalactitic formations enhanced by ingenious illuminations. Good dry floor and ample headroom contribute to the enjoyment of a tour of these remarkable caverns.' Am I the only one to think that perhaps it was more of an adventure in 1920 than it is today?

It is obvious that on leaving Stump Cross Caverns the friends continued along the road as far as Hebden, but whether or not one would choose to do this today is highly debatable. As far as the steep descent to Dibble's Bridge the road is quite wide with good grass verges but from the bridge onwards the road is much narrower and verges almost non-existent. The alternative is to continue along the road from the caverns as far as a junction just beyond Fancarl House (GR.071631). The narrow road to the left is signposted to Barden, Appletreewick and Burnsall. By following this for about three-quarters of a mile to the point where it bears sharply to the left, then for another 200 yards, there will be seen a signpost to

Linton Church.

Hartlington. This track provides an easy descent of some 1³/₄ miles to rejoin the road one has recently left. By crossing the road to Woodhouse Farm there, once again, is the Dales Way on which this tour of the dales commenced. From thereon, the route to Grassington needs little comment.

Arriving at the picturesque village of Burnsall, where refreshments may be obtained, the Dales Way switches to the opposite side of the River Wharfe until the Hebden suspension foot bridge is reached. On crossing this, one can either visit Hebden itself, although the C.H.A. Hostel at which the Sturdy Tramps were refreshed no longer exists, or immediately turn left and continue along the Dales Way which quite literally follows the course of the river, unlike the upper reaches between Kettlewell and Buckden. Horace Pawson gives the impression that the friends visited the 11th Century Church of St. Michael at Linton and in order to do this they could have crossed the river by stepping stones. In theory and according to the O.S. map, these are still accessible from the Dales Way, but in practice the river would have to be at an extremely low level if the crossing was to be attempted today. Even so, a number of the stones appear to have disappeared altogether. But the simple, low-lying church which serves the four communities of Linton, Hebden, Grassington and Threshfield is well worth visiting although by the more conventional route after crossing the Wharfe by the footbridge at Linton Falls. The present, attractive wooden footbridge was erected in 1989 to replace a metal structure which had become dangerous. It is the fourth bridge to span the river at this spot, the initial purpose being to provide easy access for people from Grassington who worked at the mill, the site of which is now occupied by the recently built riverside dwellings. The weir and sluice gate which originally controlled the flow of water to a waterwheel are still in evidence.

For the present day wanderer, there is no train to catch as did the Sturdy Tramps in 1920. The Yorkshire Dales Line from Skipton to Grassington opened in July, 1902, but the passenger service was withdrawn in September, 1930. The station was actually at Threshfield and not Grassington itself. Today, unlike that in Wensleydale, the line is still in operation for mineral traffic only as far as the large limestone quarry one passes on the roadside on leaving Threshfield in the Skipton direction. So, those of you who have come this far on foot and not merely in thought or the reading of the written word, retrace your steps from the church, over the footbridge and up the narrow, well-trodden lane to the bus terminus in Grassington where, if you are fortunate, you may just be in time to catch a bus to your homeward destination!

To write any more would be superfluous, for this commentary is intended merely to complement that which was written more than seventy years ago. Therefore return to Horace Pawson's own conclusion and let that stand as a reminder that in our sophisticated, technological lives, great pleasure, satisfaction and peace of mind are to be found in what Nature has provided on our very doorstep.

BIBLIOGRAPHY AND OTHER REFERENCES

'Countrygoer in the Dales.' Jessica Lofthouse.

'Dales Way Route Guide with Associated Walks.'
Arthur Gemmell & Colin Speakman.

Footpath Maps and Guides. Arthur Gemmell:
(a) Aysgarth Area.
(b) Grassington and District.
(c) Hawes and District.
(d) Upper Swaledale.

'Pateley Bridge & Nidderdale Official Guide.'
Pateley Bridge & Nidderdale Chamber of Trade.

'Roads & Trackways of the Yorkshire Dales.' Geoffrey N. Wright.

'Richmond Town Trail.' Richmondshire District Council.

'The Coast to Coast Walk.' Alfred Wainwright.

'The Nidd Valley Light Railway.' D. J. Croft.

'The Pennine Dales.' Arthur Raistrick.

'The Railways of Craven.' Donald Binns.

'Walks in Swaledale.' Geoffrey White.

'Yorkshire Dales National Park.' Tony Waltham.
(Countryside Commission Official Guide.)